MARKETS WE THOUGHT
WE KNEW

CONSUMER CORNER SERIES
UNCONVENTIONAL LESSONS FROM
CONSUMER BEHAVIOR

Why do consumers make the choices they do, and what can those choices teach us? The Consumer Corner series explores the subtle forces that shape consumer behavior, across topics that range from food, retail, health, vacations, and more. By spotlighting overlooked, counterintuitive, or nontraditional insights, the series challenges standard economic thinking and highlights the messy, human side of decision-making that sometimes occurs when humans engage in the marketplace. Drawing on behavioral science, lived experiences, and industry expertise, this series reveals what people can teach us as they make complex choices across the supply chain.

SERIES EDITOR

Nicole J. Olynk Widmar
Professor and Head of the Department Agricultural Economics
Purdue University

OTHER TITLES IN THIS SERIES

Decisions That Shape Supply Chains

MARKETS WE THOUGHT WE KNEW

NICOLE J. OLYNK WIDMAR
MICHAEL L. SMITH
ERIN ROBINSON

Purdue University Press
West Lafayette, Indiana

CONTENTS

INTRODUCTION

Markets We Thought We Knew

Adam Smith's *The Wealth of Nations* (1776) introduced the concept of the "invisible hand," in which individuals who act in their own best interest ultimately benefit society in its entirety through the workings of a free market. Smith said, "By pursuing his own interest he frequently promotes that of the society more effectually than when he really intends to promote it." Fundamentally, the free market allows for individuals to be motivated to produce or sell what others want to buy, which should lead to efficient allocations of resources. By following what individuals want to buy and using that as a guide for what individuals are willing to sell, society benefits on the whole. In essence, a self-interested individual can be thought of as being guided through market interactions as if being helped by an "invisible hand," hence the coining of the concept.

The "invisible hand" concept remains a valid and useful idea. Markets work to incentivize provision of what people need and want, to create competition, to promote efficiency, and to create a stream of new and innovative goods and services for societies. The idea works best when the market is entirely free to operate, and it does so without friction. In reality, we have frictions and a variety of factors that commonly lead to market failures. We also have the policies, regulations, and laws that govern societies and intentionally alter the function of markets for a variety of reasons. We can argue about how one society or another chooses to govern, or even interfere in more directly, various markets. Regardless of reason, intent, or how it plays out in practice, all these various interferences change what would have happened if the market were free. Markets do not operate in isolation from other markets, nor do markets in one society operate in isolation from markets in another. We then have black markets for illegal goods or services, which operate outside of legal boundaries (but operate nonetheless).

Simply stated, the market is a mechanism through which buyers and sellers interact—physically, virtually, or some combination of both—to determine the price at which goods, services, or assets can be exchanged. While the market for corn, for example, is easy to visualize (though still complex in construction and operation), other markets are harder to envision, such as those for intangible assets. There are entire markets for intangibles that require validation of the asset's existence in a way that all parties involved trust and accept before an exchange is possible: for example, trademarks, import quotas, production quotas, and marketing rights. Markets can be as simple as a single location where goods are visible and can be carried home upon purchase, or as complex as the markets for cryptocurrencies. And then there is the labor market, which is commonly talked about and near and dear to most of us. In truth, we have never had just a single market operating in isolation, but a system of markets operating simultaneously within a series of policies, infrastructures, and social relations that comprise economies. These economies then interact with others to form complicated webs of relationships that direct the movement of goods, services, and assets.

Markets get blamed for a lot of things when they're down and credited for things when they're up. But we seldom stop to think about down (or up) for whom—buyer or seller? Which market? We hear phrases such as "markets do not like uncertainty," which imply that markets have feelings. They don't—although they do reflect the feelings, beliefs, expectations, and experiences of the individuals participating in them. If sellers of product Y all become concerned that demand for product Y is about to rise or fall dramatically, then the price for product Y is likely to change based on those expectations. Simply stated, the market will have priced in an expectation. Whether those expectations ever come to fruition is a different discussion. Still, markets react to a variety of factors, and understanding how different markets react to different things becomes important for managers, government leaders, policy makers, and a wide variety of other roles in societies. Beyond general movements up or down, we want to understand patterns, reactions, and corrections over time. There is great interest in how different markets behave during changes in demand, supply, and policy—and in how they handle external shocks. Each day, and even within a single day, buyers and sellers reach agreements on the prices at which items, services, assets, or pieces of information are exchanged. If everyone wants crop X and is willing to pay more and more for crop X, then resources will flow toward the production of more crop X. This resource movement toward more valuable uses is the market in action. But does the market always work?

As with most things, there is a gap between theory and reality when it comes to how markets function and behave. In practice, many (most, if not all) markets operate with some degree of efficiency loss. This may be due to communication frictions, unequal access to information, or simply transaction costs. In an oversimplified explanation, markets can be said to fail, or falter, when they do not allocate resources efficiently or do not to lead to the best possible outcome for a society. A variety of reasons for market failures are outlined in microeconomics textbooks, most of which exist to some degree in real-world markets. Economists focus on externalities, market power (like oligopolies or monopolies), informational asymmetries, incomplete markets, failures to behave rationally or make individual optimal decisions, and transaction costs. Beyond these reasons, public goods pose a major challenge for markets. For example, national security or clean air are goods that are nonrival and nonexcludable—everyone benefits, and it's hard to prevent someone from doing so. Thus, these goods are not easily allocated through markets and represent perhaps the clearest and most cited examples of when markets fail.

When we consider food and agricultural markets specifically, there is a heightened level of interest. Food is necessary and life-sustaining. While individuals' specific preferences may vary, a base level of demand is fixed—people must eat. Agricultural markets, therefore, are generally underpinned by this necessity.

1

KNOW YOUR DAIRY CUSTOMERS

BY CHRISTOPHER A. WOLF

Consumers are increasingly interested in the methods employed in food production, especially as it relates to livestock, dairy, and poultry. As a result, commercial agriculture is facing increased pressure to adopt changes to production processes. This pressure for changes often relates to how the product is made—such as treatment of the cow—rather than the output characteristics, such as the milk or meat itself.

With the increasing interconnectedness, communication, and publicity available through social media, coupled with the lack of experience and knowledge typical US consumers have regarding agriculture, production practices on farms have been under scrutiny in some quarters. This increased scrutiny brings both costs and benefits. Let's consider some of the lessons we have learned through research on consumer perceptions and demands for dairy products as they relate to production characteristics. In general, research suggests that while most people claim to care a great deal about production practices, relatively few are willing to pay extra for products that align with those practices.

Let us begin with some noncontroversial statements about consumer demands:

- Consumers want to trust their food supply in several dimensions, including safety, ethics, sustainability, and so on.
- Consumers want to avoid feeling guilty about their food choices.

To avoid regulation, producers must maintain social trust. Social trust is the acceptance of a business or industry's operational practices by the public and relevant stakeholders. Without social license, the industry ends up regulated, monitored, and/or litigated to enforce compliance with laws and expectations. Traditionally, farmers and agriculture have been trusted and admired.

Farm production practices evolve through one of three avenues: regulation, markets, or voluntary industry initiatives. Regulation includes legislation or ballot initiatives. The market is manifested through retailers or processors encouraging or requiring change. Retailers often mandate these changes due to pressure from interested parties or advocacy groups and to help bolster corporate image and value. The final method is when producers voluntarily adopt, confirm, or verify production practice changes to maintain trust, social license and market access, and in some cases, receive price premiums.

Potential solutions to avoid regulation and maintain social license include the use of process labels, consumer education, and voluntary certification programs. Process labels describe how animals are raised, crops are grown, or ingredients are processed. Examples include rBST-free, grass-fed, and antibiotic-free. These labels often emphasize what was *not* done during production. Advantages of labels include providing information, enhancing consumer trust, and assisting in market segmentation.

However, labels also present many disadvantages, including the following:

- Potential information overload, where additional information can be distracting and complicate decisions
- Confusion and misperception
- Elevated food safety and risk perceptions

- Negative reactions to the disclosure of production technology or practices
- Decreased demand for safe products
- Added labeling costs
- Potential reductions in agricultural productivity

One solution frequently proposed is educational programs for the general public to understand modern agriculture. The primary advantage of educational programs is that few people have much context for production agriculture (fewer than 2 percent of US citizens are farmers). There is some evidence that education can improve understanding. The disadvantages are that people must be willing to be educated, and even when educated, consumers still lack the broader context necessary to understand accepted industry practices. Additionally, misinformation or poor framing can lead education efforts to work against intended goals.

Increasingly, farm groups are adopting voluntary programs that include standards, verification, and certification. The Farmers Assuring Responsible Management (FARM) program is a good example. Consumer acceptance of these programs depends largely on certification, with the majority of consumers preferring USDA certification. Consumers generally do not trust industries to police themselves. Also, in order to maintain trust, violations of standards need real consequences as the entire industry is injured when a public incident occurs.

Most consumers indicate a willingness to pay premiums for animal welfare practices and other production factors. Sometimes the result is actually a premium for providing these practices, while other times it is a discount for failing to provide practices, assurances, or verification. The current dairy industry market is not really structured to return premiums to the farm level. Thus, one likely outcome is that premiums will evolve into discounts or limited market access.

Implications for dairy producers and cooperatives are as follows:

- Get ahead on animal welfare market and policy issues. Set the tone and drive the conversation.
- Make education available but realize participation may be limited.

- Police yourself. Incidents cost everyone—not just the offending operation.
- Third-party verification has value.

Adapted from original posting as *ConsumerCorner.2020.Letter.05* (https://agribusiness.purdue.edu/consumer_corner/know-your-dairy -customers/)

2

CONSUMER PREFERENCES FOR LAYING HEN HOUSING

BY COURTNEY BIR

Eggs get a lot of attention—and for good reason. They've long been a relatively cheap source of protein, commonly eaten for breakfast in the United States and a key ingredient in many other dishes. Eggs are also a healthful and highly valued item in children's diets. Given their popularity, production practices related to laying hens have been a point of contention. This is especially true in states where they have proposed or passed legislation related to animal welfare.

A recent collaboration broached the subject of what consumers want in egg production, just beginning to answer one question about consumer demand and perceptions: Which egg laying hen cage type best fits consumer preferences?

We evaluated three housing options, approaching the topic from several different perspectives:

- Enriched colony systems: These house sixty to 250 hens in larger-than-conventional cages equipped with perches, nesting areas, and materials to facilitate foraging and dust bathing. These systems can house up to 100,000 or more hens in each building.

- Aviary (cage-free) housing: These aviary (AV) systems allow hens to roam throughout various sized sections of a building. Each section of an AV housing system contains perches, nesting areas, and dust-bathing material. There can be up to 80,000 or more hens per building.
- Conventional cage housing: These traditional setups house four to nine hens. The approximate space per hen is eighty square inches. A single building may hold thousands of cages, totaling as many as 200,000 hens.

STUDY 1 (OCHS ET AL. 2018)

The question: What is the alignment between consumers' beliefs about what a cage type provides and what the cage actually provided?

THE STATS:

- Nationally representative online survey of 2,813 people
- Methods: Likert scale and simple survey questions
- We asked people whether they thought cage type had a positive, negative, or no impact on hen health and stress, hen behavior, environmental impact, natural resource use efficiency, worker health and safety, food safety, and food quality. We then compared their answers to documented impacts.

THE FINDINGS:

People were at least somewhat honest. When asked to rate their knowledge level about farming practices in egg production (on a scale from 1 = extremely unknowledgeable to 5 = extremely knowledgeable), 46 percent rated themselves a 2 or lower, while 31 percent considered themselves neutral. Only 5.6 percent of respondents correctly indicated that free-range negatively impacted hen health and stress when compared to conventional

TABLE 2.1. *Percentage of Respondents Who Gave the Correct Answer on Impacts by Housing Type*

ATTRIBUTE	FREE-RANGE	CAGE-FREE AVIARY	ENRICHED COLONY
Hen health and stress	5.6% (Negative)	6.9% (Negative)	30.5% (No Impact)
Hen behavior	74.1% (Positive)	71.6% (Positive)	57.2% (Positive)
Environmental impact	NA	6.9% (Negative)	50.3% (Positive)
Natural resource use efficiency	NA	7.2% (Negative)	38.5% (No Impact)
Worker health and safety	NA	6.6% (Negative)	45.2% (No Impact)
Food safety	32.7% (No Impact)	33.4% (No Impact)	39.7% (No Impact)
Egg quality	25.7% (No Impact)	28.1% (No Impact)	35.9% (No Impact)

cage housing. On a more positive note, 57 percent of respondents correctly identified that enriched colonies had a positive impact on hen behavior.

THE TAKE-HOME MESSAGE:

The US public perceives cage-free aviaries as achieving essentially the same positive impact on hen health and stress, hen behavior, environmental impact, and other important attributes as eggs produced in free-range systems. Most respondents did not recognize the potential for a negative impact on worker health and safety and hen health and stress from the transition from conventional cages to alternative housing systems.

STUDY 2 (OCHS ET AL. 2019)

THE QUESTION:

What attributes do people feel are most important when purchasing eggs?

THE STATS:

- Nationally representative online survey of 2,574 people
- Methods: Likert scale (rate importance on a scale from 1 to 5); forced ranking (order attributes from most to least important); and best-worst scaling (choose the most and least important attribute several times to determine overall relative importance)
- Attributes studied were hen health and safety, mortality, foot condition, behavior, stress, cannibalism/aggression, and feather condition using all of these methods.

THE FINDINGS:

When respondents used a Likert scale, there were a lot of ties for what mattered most—no surprise, since they didn't have to make tradeoffs. They can say they want everything! There was more variation in rank using the forced rank and best-worst scaling methods.

TABLE 2.2. *Ranking of Laying Hen Production Attributes by Methods*

ATTRIBUTE	LIKERT SCALE	FORCED RANK	BEST-WORST SCALING
Hen mortality	1	3	1
Hen foot condition	1	6	6
Hen behavior	1	1	1
Hen stress	1	1	1
Hen cannibalism/aggression	1	5	4
Hen feather condition	7	7	7
Worker health and safety	1	4	7

THE TAKE-HOME MESSAGE:

There are many differences based on the method used. Different methods tell different stories, but overall, the most important laying hen welfare attributes for the average US consumer were hen behavior, hen stress, and hen mortality. Cannibalism/aggression and worker health and safety landed in the middle. Feather and foot condition mattered the least.

Interestingly, consumer preferences best align with enriched colony housing. This is at odds with the perceived consumer/interest group preference for free-range housing.

STUDY 3 (WOLF ET AL. 2019)

THE QUESTION:

What are respondents willing to pay for different housing types and other egg attributes? Housing types included were aviary, enriched colony, and conventional. Other attributes included were size, color, and verifier.

THE STATS:

- Nationally representative online survey of 2,813 respondents
- Method: Willingness-to-pay (WTP) choice experiment
- Some respondents received an informational treatment explaining housing types to allow evaluation of whether it changed people's preferences.

THE FINDINGS:

Respondents who saw videos showing and describing hen housing systems were willing to pay $0.50/dozen less for the cage-free aviary housing when compared to conventional cages. Of those who saw the video, people were willing to pay $0.51 less for a brown egg than a white egg.

Verification mattered too. People were willing to pay a positive amount for all verification entities studied when compared to no verification. When attributes such as housing type or other production practices aren't easily observed by the end consumer, verification of attributes can become more important. Respondents were willing to pay a negative or zero amount for medium, extra-large, and jumbo eggs compared to large eggs. The opt-out variable captures the level of discomfort a respondent feels when unable to purchase their preferred eggs—essentially, that "oh shucks" moment when you leave the store empty-handed, expressed in dollar terms.

TABLE 2.3. *Willingness to Pay (WTP) for Laying Hen Production Attributes*

VARIABLE	WTP/DOZEN VIDEO, N = 1,353	WTP/DOZEN NO VIDEO, N = 1,460
Enriched colony	$0.52*	$0.7*
Cage-free aviary	$0.51*	$1.01*
Brown	-$0.23*	-$0.13*
USDA verification	$1.16*	$0.91*
Third-party verification	$0.61*	$0.43*
Industry verification	$0.77*	$0.56*
Size medium	-$0.25	-$0.27
Size extra-large	-$0.06	-$0.08
Size jumbo	$0	$0.04
Opt-out	-$5.67*	-$5.23*

* The WTP is statistically different between those who saw the info shock video and those who did not.

THE TAKE-HOME MESSAGE:

Those consumers who are uninformed about hen housing systems are willing to pay more for "cage-free" eggs, even if the actual welfare benefits aren't clear to them. Education could change that willingness—and maybe even lead to savings at the checkout line.

GENERAL CONCLUSIONS

- Read studies carefully. What's the sample, and what can it really say? Did they take precautions to minimize bias and ensure data quality?
- It takes a lot of methods and a lot of work to answer even "easy" or small consumer questions.
- Consumers evolve. For example, the COVID-19 pandemic likely shifted preferences as more people cooked at home instead of dining

out. This change means that these food-related preferences and attitudes are probably ripe for reevaluation.

WORKS CITED

Ochs, D., Wolf, C., Widmar, N. J., and Bir, C. 2018. "Consumer Perceptions of Egg-Laying Hen Housing Systems." *Poultry Science* 97(10): 3390–96. https://doi.org/10.3382/ps/pey205.

Ochs, D., Wolf, C., Widmar, N. J. O., and Bir, C. 2019. "Is There a 'Cage-Free' Lunch in US Egg Production? Public Views of Laying Hen Housing Attributes." *Journal of Agricultural and Resource Economics* 44(2): 345–61.

Wolf, C., Ochs, D., Bir, C., Lai, J., and Widmar, N. J. O. 2019. "Hen Housing System Information Effects on U.S. Egg Demand." *Food Policy* 87:101743. https://doi.org/10.1016/j.foodpol.2019.101743.

Adapted from original posting as *ConsumerCorner.2020.Article.04* (https://agribusiness.purdue.edu/consumer_corner/customer -preferences-for-laying-hen-housing/)

3

THE "TRUTH" ABOUT GLUTEN

BY BAILEY NORWOOD

I s gluten bad for you? At one point, evidence suggested that some non–celiac disease patients experienced digestive discomfort when consuming gluten. However, further studies showed this is not the case. The medical profession remains uncertain whether gluten sensitivity is an actual condition for some people, yet surveys show that 15 percent of Americans claim to be gluten sensitive (table 3.1). Moreover, while the medical profession does not consider foods containing gluten to be less healthy for the general population than their gluten-free counterparts, 23 percent of Americans believe that avoiding gluten is part of maintaining good health. Many even report weight loss on a gluten-free diet, despite no inherent link between eliminating gluten and weight loss.

TABLE 3.1. *Attitudes Toward Gluten Held by a Representative Sample of 1,000 US Citizens*

	I BELIEVE I AM SENSITIVE TO GLUTEN FOOD	AVOIDING GLUTEN IS PART OF MAINTAINING GOOD HEALTH
Agree	15%	23%
Neither	17%	42%
Disagree	68%	35%

Source: Norwood, Franklin Bailey. 2021. "Perceived Impact of Information Signals on Opinions About Gluten-Free Diets." *PLOS One.*

This must be frustrating to food companies. Gluten—a combination of two intertwined proteins—has been a staple of human diets since the Neolithic age. So pivotal is its role in Western civilization that it's played a leading part both at the dinner table and in religions. The Sumerians believed wheat was given to them by the goddess Ashnan, and the Greek city of Eleusis believed their wheat was given by Demeter. The meaning of the word "lord" is Old English for "the man who gives out bread." While religions have changed much over the millennia, wheat, rye, and barley have remained dietary cornerstones.

Why, then, are so many people turning their backs on this delicious, nutritious, and time-tested food source without any scientific evidence for doing so? One could just as easily ask why the Sumerians believed a goddess gave them wheat, and the answer lies in how people seek truth. Philosophers have many definitions of truth. One of the more popular ones is correspondence theory, which holds that a statement is deemed true if it is consistent with objective facts. This is the model of truth that gluten-free food producers employ when arguing that gluten is not unhealthy for non–celiac disease patients.

However, it only takes a modicum of reflection to recognize that we cannot rely on the correspondence theory for all our decisions. Instead, most of us employ pragmatic theory in our day-to-day decisions, which allows a statement to be considered true by its usefulness. The Sumerians presumably invented the myth of Ashnan giving them wheat because it was useful, perhaps facilitating social cohesion. Likewise, a consumer might benefit from falsely believing gluten to be unhealthy. Let's explore why.

The gluten-free diet is a pragmatic choice. The typical American diet is generally considered unhealthy for several reasons. We do not have enough diversity in our diets, we don't eat enough vegetables, and our foods are excessively high in sugar and low in fiber, just to name a few. Gluten itself is not unhealthy, but it tends to play a prominent role in many unhealthy foods. Fast-food burgers are made with bread from white flour, and while that burger itself could be part of a healthy diet, a diet consisting of mostly burgers is not healthy. Cookies, doughnuts, crackers, cake: They all contain gluten, and we are told to eat less of these foods.

When a person adopts a gluten-free diet, chances are, they are doing more than just eliminating gluten from their diet. Eliminating gluten is difficult because it is in so many food products, and eliminating it requires a more intentional attitude toward food. While the gluten-free convert may have formerly paid little attention to what they were eating, they now pay careful attention to ingredients. Thus, they are paying more attention to sugar content and fiber intake as well. Anything that encourages more mindful eating can improve health. Thus, they feel better, and though gluten may have had nothing to do with it, they attribute feeling healthy to a gluten-free diet.

Most food products containing wheat rely on white flour, which is lower in fiber than whole wheat flour. Gluten-free products often contain more unusual grains such as buckwheat, teff, and quinoa. Flour from these grains typically uses the whole seed and offers higher fiber content. Moreover, their inclusion provides a nice source of grain diversity compared to the typical American diet that includes wheat grains almost exclusively. Alternatively, people who seek alternative grains replace traditional grains with vegetables, like cauliflower for their pizza crust. While the gluten in the pizza crust was not unhealthy, its replacement with vegetables does improve health. So again, though gluten wasn't the problem, the person feels better by replacing refined flour with vegetables.

Perhaps this is best stated in the comedy movie *This Is the End*: "Whenever you feel shitty, that's 'cause of gluten. . . . Gluten's a vague term. . . . It's something used to categorize things that are bad, you know? Calories, that's a gluten. Fat, that's a gluten" (*This Is The End* 2013).

Those seeking to improve their diet likely adopt other healthy behavioral changes, like starting to exercise. By now, you're getting the point: They feel better, and though gluten had nothing to do with it, they partly attribute it to a gluten-free diet.

Is this an irrational attitude toward gluten? On the one hand, yes. It confuses correlation with causation. On the other hand, the belief that "gluten is unhealthy" led to improved health. After all, people are regularly avoiding gluten without really knowing what gluten is. Before you mock them, think about how many of your beliefs are held not because of their scientific validity, but because of their usefulness.

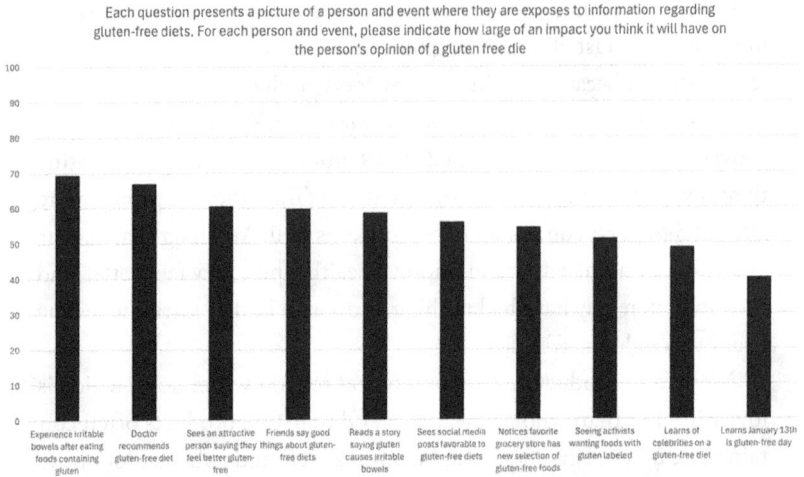

Each question presents a picture of a person and event where they are exposes to information regarding gluten-free diets. For each person and event, please indicate how large of an impact you think it will have on the person's opinion of a gluten free die

FIGURE 3.1. Predicted impact of various information signals about gluten in a representative sample of 1,317 Americans. *Source:* Norwood, Franklin Bailey. 2021. "Perceived Impact of Information Signals on Opinions About Gluten-Free Diets." *PLOS One.*

Ask yourself, where do you get your information? This is perhaps why consumers often get their health information from sources that can, from a scientific perspective, be unreliable. I recently conducted a survey of over 1,000 Americans asking them the impact they believe certain events would have on a hypothetical other person's opinion about gluten-free diets. The results are shown in figure 3.1. Not surprisingly, an unpleasant eating experience and a doctor's recommendation is projected to have the largest impact. However, hearing a friend or an attractive person say good things about a gluten-free diet has a larger impact than reading about a new study, suggesting that people are so accustomed to contradictory studies about food and health they would rather rely on the personal advice of friends. Social media is thought to have a moderate impact, and even minor events, like learning that January 13 is National Gluten-Free Day, has measurable effects. This demonstrates the wide array of sources people use to collect information to make dieting decisions, much of it deemed true because it is useful, even if scientifically untrue.

A word of advice to food manufacturers frustrated by consumers who ignore scientific consensus, especially when organizations like the CDC are distrusted. Rather than solely promoting scientific truths, companies can learn to pivot toward pragmatic truths while still honoring the scientific truth. For example, gluten is seen as unhealthy to some because they have seen documentaries saying modern wheat breeding is "industrialized," but there is nothing to stop a company from defending modern wheat while also selling flour made from heirloom varieties.

Consumers are not irrational for believing something is true simply because the belief is useful. What is irrational is for a food company to not cater to these beliefs.

WORKS CITED

Norwood, Franklin Bailey. 2021. "Perceived Impact of Information Signals on Opinions About Gluten-Free Diets." *PLOS One.*

This Is the End. 2013. Directed by Seth Rogen and Evan Goldberg.

Adapted from original posting as *ConsumerCorner.2020.Letter.27* (https://agribusiness.purdue.edu/consumer_corner/the-truth-about-gluten/)

4

WATER, WATER, EVERYWHERE . . .

BY LIXIA H. LAMBERT AND COURTNEY BIR

I t's challenging to critically consider something so familiar: water. Among all natural and environmental resources supporting life, water and air are arguably the most vital. In 1977, the United Nations declared access to clean water a fundamental human right (UN 1977). At least fifteen liters of water per person per day are required for our most basic needs to avoid health concerns (WHO 2017).

Water also serves as a production input for goods and services through both indirect and direct linkages. When and how much water is demanded for economic activities—and how economic sectors and industries have used surface and groundwater to dispose of their waste, whether intentionally or unintentionally—affect water availability and quality. For example, agricultural production may adversely affect water quality (unintentionally) and the cost is borne by society. In the United States, nutrient runoff from croplands into the Mississippi River and its tributaries is the leading cause of hypoxia in the Gulf of Mexico (Rabalais et al. 1996). This ecological disruption has impacted fisheries, consumers, and the seafood market through rising prices (Smith et al. 2017). In economics, this situation is described as a negative externality because the costs of diminished water quality are unaccounted for in the producer's use of fertilizer or animal waste disposal.

This begs the question: How do we fulfill access to safe and clean water as a human right? In the United States, the Safe Drinking Water Act (SDWA) was passed in 1976 and amended in 1986 and 1996. This legislation set legal and health standards for drinking water contaminant levels and treatment rules to protect public health under the US Environmental Protection Act (EPA) and state enforcement. There are over 148,000 public water systems in the United States. Over 90 percent of these systems rely on groundwater and the remainder on surface water. It is difficult for all public water systems to comply consistently with SDWA standards.

This brings us to another important question: What about the cost? In economic theory, a water utility company falls under the natural monopoly category. They did not choose to be a monopoly, but the single, large-scale producer is the most efficient way of providing water to households at a geographic location (a town, city, or region). Once a public water supply system is constructed and the number of homes connecting to the network increases, the average and marginal costs of water treatment, distribution, and plant maintenance decrease. This type of monopoly is allowed by the government but is regulated to ensure quality service and fair pricing. Most local governments do not allow excess profit for water utility companies beyond covering their costs.

Designing, constructing, operating, and maintaining a water supply system that distributes water to its users while meeting national safety standards can be costly. A well-structured residential water pricing scheme is a useful tool for recovering water supply systems' costs and limiting wasteful consumption. Consumers or taxpayers pay the price of infrastructure, treatment, and distribution of drinking water.

However, low-income households may be unable to pay water bills if prices are too high. Recent research on water bills in twelve major cities led by *The Guardian* found that water bills rose by at least 27 percent in major US cities, with the highest increase (154 percent) observed in Austin, Texas, between 2010 and 2018 (Colton 2020). Water utility companies may shut off water in households that do not pay their water bills on time, and the situation worsened during the COVID-19 pandemic for many families without running water. To address this issue, dozens of states mandated that public water supply systems provide access to their services during the pandemic for health reasons. Nonetheless, the question remains: If accessing clean water is a fundamental human right, what can society do to help these consumers fulfill their rights?

So, how are water resources allocated to different users and economic activities? In addition to sustaining life, water is an essential input for agriculture, manufacturing, transportation, energy production, and recreation. How we efficiently allocate water resources among these competing uses is a pressing issue in many regions, especially in water-limited areas.

In economic theory, efficient allocation of water occurs when the marginal benefit of consumption (the benefit obtained by consuming one additional unit of water) equals the marginal cost of water provision (the cost of supplying one additional unit of water). In other words, people only pay what water is worth to them. Water flows to high-value uses in society and away from low-value uses, thereby maximizing society's welfare. Ideally, markets function to achieve this win-win outcome. However, efficient allocation of water resources is difficult to achieve in most situations. Different legal and institutional frameworks govern water resources rather than markets. In practice, most water is allocated through water rights. Selling and purchasing water through markets is not the norm.

In the United States, two major doctrines govern water rights: riparian rights and prior appropriation doctrine. Riparian rights allocate the right to use water to landowners adjacent to the waterways, streams, and rivers. The rights to access water are attached to land property rights. This approach is mainly adopted in the eastern United States, where water is a relatively abundant resource. The prior appropriation doctrine—summarized by the phrase "first in time, first in right"—is more common in the West. Under the prior appropriation doctrine system, senior water rights holders have precedence during times of water scarcity. If a water right has not been used for a certain period of time, the user may lose the rights. Various state and federal laws are in place to regulate the transfer of water between users, which for some communities has led to inefficient water allocation. Although intended to promote use, the "use it or lose it" principle can discourage water conservation as owners fear losing the right to use the water.

Water trading through a well-established market can reduce water allocation inefficiency. When limited water resources do not meet all users' demands given their willingness to pay and established water rights, purchasing or selling temporary (or seasonal) water use rights could be an effective method to transfer water from low-value to high-value uses. Recent research has shown that well-functioning market institutions and low transaction costs are key drivers to increase participation in water trading markets (Wheeler and Garrick 2020).

WORKS CITED

Colton, R. D. 2020. "The Affordability of Water and Wastewater Service in Twelve US Cities: A Social, Business, and Environmental Concern." *The Guardian.*

Rabalais, N. N., R. E. Turner, D. Justić, Q. Dortch, W. J. Wiseman, and B. K. Sen Gupta. 1996. "Nutrient Changes in the Mississippi River and System Responses on the Adjacent Continental Shelf." *Estuaries*, 386–407.

Smith, M. D., A. Oglend, A. J. Kirkpatrick, F. Asche, L. S. Bennear, J. K. Craig, and J. M. Nance. 2017. "Seafood Prices Reveal Impacts of a Major Ecological Disturbance." *Proceedings of the National Academy of Sciences.* National Academy of Sciences.

United Nations. 1977. *Report of the United Nations Water Conference.* Mar del Plata.

Wheeler, S. A., and D. E. Garrick. 2020. "A Tale of Two Water Markets in Australia: Lessons for Understanding Participation in Formal Water Markets." *Oxford Review of Economic Policy*, 132–53.

WHO. (2017). *WHO 2017 Guidelines for Drinking-Water Quality, 4th ed., Incorporating the 1st Addendum.* World Health Organization. Available from: https://www.who.int/publications-detail-redirect/9789241549950.

Adapted from original postings as *ConsumerCorner.2021.Letter02* (https://agribusiness.purdue.edu/consumer_corner/water-water-everywhere/) and *ConsumerCorner.2021.Letter03* (https://agribusiness.purdue.edu/consumer_corner/allocation-of-a-paramount-resource-water/)

5

THE CURIOUS CASE
OF THE BIDET

I f you ask an economist what they actually do, you will likely hear some version of "studying decision-making under conditions of scarcity." The answer possibly includes the word "markets," too—and for good reason. Many economists study some kind of market. In what amounts to both a blessing and a curse, everyone else (with or without years of studying formal mathematical models) does the very same thing. A common critique of introductory economics classes (commonly called Principles of Economics at the college level) and the discipline itself is that we rely too heavily on mathematical arguments, seemingly contrived graphs, and an unyielding insistence on measuring everything.

In what amounts to a great boon to the usefulness of economists, markets are constantly changing. Sometimes, these changes occur rapidly and are triggered by a natural disaster or act-of-God event. In such moments, markets may face structural changes. A supply shortage or demand surge can have a harsh effect on the market's ability to deliver what consumers want or need, while maintaining incentives for the producer to keep producing. Economists might call these events exogenous shocks, or a sudden, external force that may (or may not) generate big impacts on a market.

In these moments of shock to our markets, noneconomists often lean on their own economic intuition but may fall short. Even the most accomplished economists construct models that sometimes fail to explain what unfolds in real markets. Perhaps we're well informed by memories of the last time a market shock occurred? But behavioral science tells us that our own memory can be a poor compass.

Take, for example, the early days of the COVID-19 pandemic. When news of shortages emerged, many consumers rushed to stock up on household items. Among the more notable cases: toilet paper. At the same time, speculation suggested a link between COVID-19 and gastrointestinal symptoms—a connection that may have encouraged panic buying. (To be fair, seasonal influenza can also bring GI trouble, yet it hasn't historically led to toilet paper shortages.)

Whatever the reason, the result was dramatic. Economists at North Carolina State University have documented that on April 19, 2020, nearly half of grocery stores in the United States had completely sold out of their supply of toilet paper (Moore 2020). From a traditional economic standpoint, this panic buying might appear irrational. However, this surge in demand for necessities reflected consumers preparing for the worst. This act of preparing may have helped calm the nerves of Americans, who simply needed to feel that they were doing something in the face of the looming threat of COVID-19.

Not to be outwitted by the mere supply shortage, some irrational consumers switched course by seeking substitutes. These consumers sought a more durable good that they could substitute for toilet paper: the bidet. Sales of bidets rose sharply during the early months of the pandemic (Martin 2020). Since the fear surrounding COVID-19 has subsided and life has returned to normal, the great toilet paper stockpile effort also seems to have subsided. While demand for toilet paper has since normalized, bidet sales have remained strong—even into 2024 (Maruf 2024). It seems the demand for this durable good (the bidet) has proven more, well, durable than the demand for its disposable counterpart.

Of course, not all market changes unfold so dramatically. Some changes happen slowly and more like a trickle. The bidet, for example, has lingered on the fringes of American bathroom design for decades. But over time, the emergence and adoption of new technologies begins to slowly impact a market. Consider the emergence of mobile phones. While today nearly all Americans report owning a mobile phone (Pew Research Center 2024), that was not always the case. When Pew began surveying Americans regarding mobile phone ownership in 2011, only 35 percent reported ownership of a mobile phone. You might be surprised to hear that the first mobile phone was invented decades earlier, around 1973 (Delgado 2023). Mobile phones were preceded by the "bag phone" popular in the 1980s and 1990s, and before that, the car phone, which originated in the United States in 1946.

Initial uptake of these mobile communications technologies was not swift. Researchers recognize that adoption of early technologies (like mobile phones) spreads slowly not just because the phones were expensive and bulky, but also because of social mores—our collective hesitation to accept and normalize unfamiliar technology. As mobile phones became more commonly owned and used by Americans, a powerful force known as network effects locked us into owning and relying on them. Now, it is second nature to pick up our mobile phones. We can easily access the internet and social media through our now-called smartphones, which also have sophisticated cameras, can stream music, and provide directions to wherever we wish to go. These cases of shared use and interaction increase the convenience of mobile phones and our reliance on them, generating the network effect. In short, they're indispensable.

The bidet, in contrast, does not benefit from network effects—your experience using one isn't enhanced by someone else owning one. Nonetheless, bidet sales may spread through a different mechanism: word of mouth (Maruf 2024). Try one at a friend's house, and you might just decide to install your own.

Different products behave differently. Some you use up and throw away; others you install once and use for years. You might even use your mobile phone to tell your friends about your latest bathroom upgrade. Markets, like the goods they deliver, are far from one-size-fits-all.

WORKS CITED

Delgado, Michelle. 2023. "From 'the Brick' to the iPhone, the Cellphone Celebrates 50 Years." *Smithsonian Magazine.* April 3. https://www.smithsonianmag.com /innovation/from-the-brick-to-the-iphone-the-cellphone-celebrates-50-years -180981910/.

Martin, Michael. 2020. "Bidets Gain U.S. Popularity During the Coronavirus Crisis." npr.org/2020. March 22. https://www.npr.org/2020/03/22/819891957 /bidets-gain-u-s-popularity-during-the-coronavirus-crisis.

Maruf, Ramishah. 2024. "Why Are Bidets Just Now Getting Popular in America?" *CNN.* March 24. https://www.cnn.com/2024/03/24/business/bidet-boom -america-toilets/index.html.

Moore, Andrew. 2020. "How the Coronavirus Created a Toilet Paper Shortage." cnr.ncsu.edu. May 19. https://cnr.ncsu.edu/news/2020/05/coronavirus-toilet -paper-shortage/.

Pew Research Center. 2024. "Mobile Fact Sheet." pewresearch.org. November 13. https://www.pewresearch.org/internet/fact-sheet/mobile/.

6

MUCH ADO
ABOUT DAIRY?

Ⅰn 2020, we watched the world change before our eyes as the realities of COVID-19 set in for nations across the globe. From an economics and markets perspective, its impacts linger. In milk and dairy markets, we have unique market considerations. Despite the disruption, the food system has developed and maintained resiliency, largely keeping pace on the macro level with consumer demands (though not without some pain along the way). Dairy markets, in particular, were the focus of a great deal of attention since the very earliest days of the pandemic when food service closures, especially of schools, forced a sudden reallocation of milk supplies to home-consumable products.

COVID-19 brought adjustments. We share some reflections and lingering questions.

The sudden transition to "stay at home" in mid-March 2020 led to significant changes in shopping for food at home versus away from home, which impacted every food sector in the nation and most around the world. For dairy markets, however, there was the confounding issue of movement of children home from schools. Fluid milk in schools is a significant market; one can visually see consumption of fluid milk and a variety of dairy products move in sync with the school year. Fluid milk consumption declines reported currently are attributed, at least in part, to lowered school attendance during the pandemic.

Basically overnight the demand for milk in schools fell (to near zero), leaving raw milk without a home for processing and fueling national media stories on milk dumping. While there was public outrage evident and the actual scale of milk dumping was drastically higher than usual, missing from much of the reporting was the relative localization of massive increases in dumping to the Northeast (and then Southeast, in that order).[1] Adding to the sting of dumped milk and (at the time) milk prices dropping rapidly were the images of empty supermarket dairy displays as shoppers sought but could not find fluid milk. Undoubtedly, dairy producers and the dairy industry faced some dark times in March–May 2020, as did many industries and societies grappling with COVID-19.

Certainly, nobody wants to see milk dumped; there is an emotional response to seeing what we recognize as a wholesome, complete food, often in the context of infants and children, wasted. However, what was largely missing from media coverage was the resilience shown by the milk supply and processing chain in the recovery/adjustments that followed. Considering the scale and speed of the adjustments necessary, the industry response was impressive. The duration when milk processing was unavailable for raw product was reasonably short-lived as the U.S. dairy industry worked to redirect product for processing, which includes a "heavy lift" in terms of logistics of a perishable product requiring refrigeration combined with processing capacity and packaging availability. There was a brief period of time during which retail supermarkets struggled to keep fluid milk stocked on shelves as U.S. households moved home and stocked up on staple products. The transition to supplying more fluid milk for home consumption and less to restaurant and food service (including schools) was rapid, and the supply chain showed resiliency, although admittedly not without some short-term adjustment pain.

Dairy consumption at home is simply different than in restaurants or food-service establishments for most U.S. consumers. Consumption of butter and cheeses are of particular interest in the food at home versus away from home discussion. Bread baskets with butter, cream and butter-based sauces and the inclusion of items like cheeses and sour cream in dishes all tend to be more common in restaurant dishes or other "splurge" type meals than everyday at-home meals. In a special report on eating out expenditures during COVID-19 by USDA, ERS it was reported that, "In April and May 2020, food-away-from-home spending was down 50.8 and 37.2 percent, respectively, when compared to the same months one year ago." Certainly the shift away from restaurant meals has changed how U.S. consumers eat. Butter stocks remain reasonably high presently, placing downward pressure on butter prices. Pizza is one of the biggest uses of mozzarella cheese in the U.S. marketplace, which is an interesting food category during the pandemic as it remained reasonably in-demand as a take-out item, even as households continue to stay at home and many continue to avoid in-person dining, even when it is available. Contrary to trends for a variety of cheese products, American-type cheeses have experienced an increase in demand during the COVID-19 era. Increased demand for American-type cheeses is fueled by at-home cooking and consumption, largely believed to be in conjunction with preparation of common comfort food items, such as macaroni and cheese. (Widmar 2020)

So what happened next? Human behavior is sticky. We did not immediately revert to old habits, even once it was possible to do so safely. Vaccines offered a spot of hope, but new variants and rollout challenges prolonged uncertainty. By early 2021, we had spent months (if not over a year) under duress, and that anxiety-driven stockpiling of canned food and toilet paper echoes Depression-era stockpiling or postwar shopping behaviors. These behavior changes persist well into recovery phases.

Even today, we continue to measure the impact this pandemic had on how we spend, save, eat, travel, and prioritize our time. How quickly some things move to find their "new normal" depends a great deal on successful vaccination programs and economic recovery around the globe.

NOTE

1. https://ag.purdue.edu/commercialag/home/paer-article/the-dairy-marketplace-reflections-on-2020-and-factors-to-watch-in-2021/#.

WORK CITED

Widmar, N. J. 2020. *The Dairy Marketplace: Reflections on 2020 and Factors to Watch in 2021.* Purdue Agricultural Economic Report.

————————

Adapted from original posting as *ConsumerCorner.2021.Letter.07* (https://agribusiness.purdue.edu/consumer_corner/much-ado-about-dairy/)

7

WHICH LOCAL PRODUCTS RESONATE MOST WITH INDIANA CONSUMERS?

BY TAYLOR THOMPSON

I n recent years—especially amid the upheaval of national food supply chains during the acute phases of COVID-19 and in the subsequent recovery period—interest in local production and processing has surged. This attention adds to an already rich and growing body of literature about local foods. Americans seemingly love local foods, yet just as quickly object, crying "Not in My Backyard" (NIMBY) when we notice the negative externalities that accompany local production. This offers the ultimate example of the production paradox: We support the concept until we catch a whiff of the reality.

To better understand how important purchasing local products is to Indiana residents, we conducted a survey in April 2021, asking participants to agree or disagree with statements involving food purchases. The statements involved specific products a consumer might encounter alongside stated preferences and values. A total of 484 completed responses were collected. The sample was targeted to be demographically representative of the Indiana population by sex, age, income, and region across the state's twelve designated Economic Development Regions.

How much do you agree or disagree with the following statements?

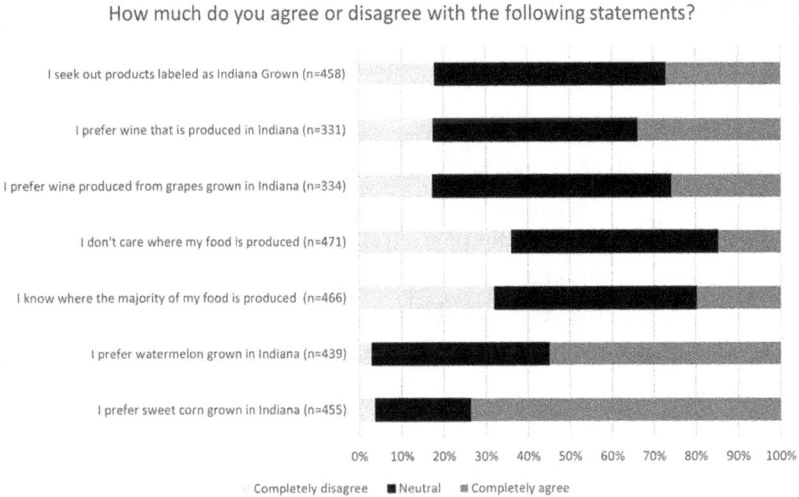

FIGURE 7.1. Preferences for Locally Grown Products Among Indiana Consumers

Respondents were given the option to select "Does not apply" or "I do not buy this product at all" in response to the seven statements studied. Responses excluding those who self-selected "Does not apply" or "I do not buy this product at all" were analyzed and are presented in figure 7.1.

Starting generally, participants had the option of selecting whether they cared (or not) about the origin of their food. Only 15 percent of responses reflected that these individuals "completely agreed" with the statement "I don't care where my food comes from." The majority, 49 percent, were neutral on the matter. Seventy-four percent of respondents "completely agreed" with the statement "I prefer sweet corn grown in Indiana." Similarly, 55 percent reported a preference for watermelon grown in Indiana.

Wine produced in Indiana and wine made from grapes in Indiana were both less preferred at 34 percent and 26 percent, respectively, than sweet corn and watermelon. Notably, the sample size analyzed for wine and grapes was significantly smaller (n = 331 and n = 334) than those for corn (n = 455) and watermelon (n = 439), indicating fewer of our respondents were active consumers of those products.

There are a few takeaways that emerge from these preliminary results. First, Indiana consumers appear to care—to an extent—about whether their food is grown in Indiana. Second, they seem familiar with Indiana's hallmark agricultural products. Indiana is well known for its corn production, generally speaking, and ranks sixth nationally in watermelon production. Overall, preliminary findings suggest Indiana residents have some understanding of the state's agricultural layout. This familiarity may influence consumer preferences, but it doesn't necessarily mean that people do extensive research before making food purchases.

It's possible that recognition plays a role. Products like corn may be more easily identified as locally grown because they're visible in local fields or sold at roadside stands. Word of mouth and familiarity with local farms or pick-your-own operations may also reinforce preferences.

We're continuing our analysis and diving deeper into the data to understand more about what local products people want and attempting to shed some light on the reasons why. As interest in local food systems remains high in post-pandemic consumer culture, understanding these dynamics will be important for farmers, marketers, and policymakers alike.

Adapted from original posting as *ConsumerCorner.2021.Letter.19* (https://agribusiness.purdue.edu/consumer_corner/which-local -products-resonate-most-with-indiana-consumers/)

8

CHICKEN WINGS COME FROM ACTUAL CHICKENS

C hicken wings are a staple in bars, restaurants, and even an entire restaurant theme with an increasing number of chains devoted to this beloved cut. Chicken wings began their rise to stardom in 1964, when the first hot wings were served at the Anchor Bar in Buffalo, New York. Since then, the humble chicken wing has gone national—and, arguably, global.

As meat consumers, we tend to focus on a very small number of products or cuts from the whole carcass and seldom mention the rest. Some of what gets spotlighted depends on the retail channel we are most familiar with or participating in presently. There's also significant seasonality at play: ham at Easter, beef tenderloin at Christmas, turkey for Thanksgiving, chicken wings for the Super Bowl and March Madness. The problem, of course, is that chicken wings don't just materialize—they come from whole chickens.

From a livestock-processing perspective, it seems simple and obvious. But from a market perspective, this is a challenge. Consumer demand differs for individual products or cuts of meat. They don't demand "chickens," they demand chicken wings. Or bacon. The livestock supply chain cannot provide more bacon without providing more of everything else that comes from a pig. Meat is a complicated market in this way; you can't make more of one cut without making more of others. And while you're attempting to meet demand for one meat product, you're potentially oversupplying another. Chicken wings aren't widgets. You can't make more chicken wings without making more chicken, no matter how important it is that you order chicken wings on Super Bowl Sunday. You also can't make more chicken breasts without making more wings, even if those wings were left uneaten in March 2020 due to COVID-19 adjustments.

Chicken wing prices collapsed during the very early weeks of the COVID-19 pandemic. As public gatherings screeched to a halt, demand for restaurant-centric foods plummeted. Chicken wings were left languishing in freezers nationwide. Headlines captured the moment: "An Unlikely Side Effect of Coronavirus: A National Surplus of Chicken Wings" (Boggage 2020). At that point, my read on the market was that we love wings, but we tend to love them in restaurants and other public/ social settings more than buying them for at-home cooking alone. With no social gatherings, no crowds, and no sports bar viewing nights, chicken wing prices fell to levels not seen since September 2011.

Then, they rallied back to normal and just kept climbing. Then came the headlines arguing that demand was incredibly strong and prices were high, but that we're not in a state of actual "shortage" (Finney 2021). By April 2021, one year after the collapse, the pendulum swung in the opposite direction. Wholesale chicken wing prices fell in March/April 2020, coinciding with closures, and then surged in 2021. In just twelve months, we went from abundant supply alongside falling prices to wanting more alongside rapidly rising prices. Given that we know there were production challenges during this COVID-19 era due to shutdowns and plant closures, it is worth noting that chicken production itself was impacted in the spring of 2020.

According to USDA-ERS (2022a, 2022b), wholesale chicken wing prices began rising as cold storage inventories started to fall. We were quite literally eating through our reserves. By 2021, stocks of chicken in cold storage were below average, contributing to upward price pressure.

Wholesale wing prices peaked at $3.25 per pound in May 2021, which was the same month cold storage levels began to recover. By January 2022,

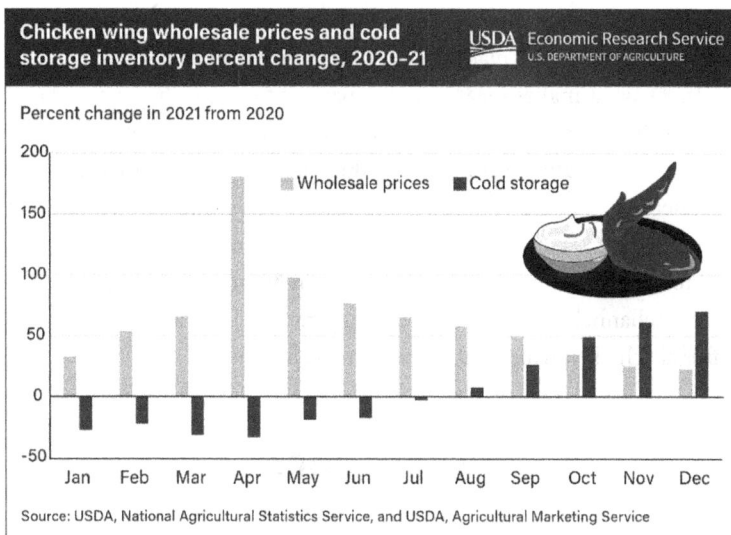

Chicken wing wholesale prices and cold storage inventory percent change, 2020-21

USDA Economic Research Service
U.S. DEPARTMENT OF AGRICULTURE

FIGURE 8.1. Wholesale chicken wing prices peaked in May 2021 as cold storage levels began to recover. *Source:* U.S. Department of Agriculture, Economic Research Service, "Wholesale Chicken Wing Prices Peaked in May 2021 as Cold Storage Levels Began to Recover," March 11, 2022.

they declined to an average of $2.68 per pound—still $0.24 higher than the previous January, but down a full $0.49 from the 2021 peak price.

Whole chicken prices showed another layer of this puzzle. After the pandemic hit in Q1 2020, whole broiler prices remained below average for nearly the entire year. Prices of chicken breasts—more directly comparable to chicken wing prices in consumer demand terms—also fell initially in response to the March 2020 domestic pandemic onset, then recovered rapidly before settling in just below the five-year average for 2015–2019. Chicken breast prices in 2021 had climbed significantly, providing evidence of strong demand and relative market scarcity, although their trend didn't mirror wing prices during this same time period.

In many ways, this is the meat market doing what economics says it should: Falling inventories lead to rising prices. But individual products/cuts like chicken wings aren't so simple. We can't directly respond to a change in demand for chicken wings without altering the supply of everything else that comes from a chicken. The chicken wing may be the star of your game-day platter, but it doesn't arrive on its own.

That's what makes meat product markets biologically governed and inherently different. Given the importance of meat and protein markets and the complicating factors surrounding meeting demand for individual products, continuous monitoring and study is warranted. During this period of rapid economic recovery with movement back into restaurants and food service, meat markets face pressure to provide specific items to specific channels at specific times (Boggage 2020). Easier said than done. After all, chicken wings come from actual chickens.

WORKS CITED

Boggage, Jacob. 2020. "An Unlikely Side Effect of Coronavirus: A National Surplus of Chicken Wings." washingtonpost.com/business. April 8. https://www .washingtonpost.com/business/2020/04/08/chicken-wings-coronavirus -march-madness/.

Finney, Mike. 2021. "High Demand During COVID Leads to Wing Shortage in Delaware." https://www.usnews.com/news/best-states/delaware/articles/2021 -05-16/high-demand-during-covid-leads-to-wing-shortage-in-delaware.

USDA, Economic Research Service. 2022a. Charts of Note. By Grace Grossen. 3/11/2022. https://www.ers.usda.gov/data-products/charts-of-note/chart-detail ?chartId=103459#:~:text=Their%20popularity%20as%20a%20takeout,and %20Poultry%20Outlook%2C%20February%202022.

USDA, Economic Research Service. 2022b. Livestock, Dairy, and Poultry Outlook. February 2022. Available at https://www.ers.usda.gov/publications/pub -details?pubid=103283.

Adapted from original posting as *ConsumerCorner.2021.Letter.20* (https://agribusiness.purdue.edu/consumer_corner/market -complication-chicken-wings-come-from-actual-chickens/)

9

WHAT'S STOPPING YOU FROM BUYING LOCAL?

BY BEN ELLMAN

I n the midst of a global health crisis that stressed agricultural supply chains, disrupted processing facilities, and sent consumers into a
full-blown toilet-paper panic, questions have been raised regarding the
increased interest in local production and processing (Goldy et al. 2020).
After all, if you couldn't count on your grocery store to have eggs, why not
turn to the farm down the road?

To explore this growing curiosity, we surveyed 484 Indiana residents
by asking them to agree or disagree with a series of statements regarding
their food purchasing to yield insight into their preferences for locally produced products. The sample was collected in April 2021 and respondents
were targeted to be representative of the Indiana population in terms of
age, sex, income, and geographic region.

As discussed in chapter 7, Indiana residents seem to care about whether
their food is local and whether they know where it came from. Seemingly contradictory to these findings, respondents generally did not know
where the majority of their purchased food originated. If locally produced food is important to Indiana residents, what prevents them from
taking a more active role in buying local products? Well, for a representative sample of Indiana residents, it was most commonly seasonality, price,
and limited selection.

TABLE 9.1. *Possible Factors Limiting Local Food Purchasing*

	VERY LIMITING	MODERATELY LIMITING	NOT LIMITING
Seasonality	41%	45%	14%
Price	34%	47%	19%
Unavailable/limited selection	26%	52%	22%
Farmer market days	27%	47%	25%
Variety	18%	51%	30%
Lacking storage or refrigeration	26%	42%	32%
Product quality	23%	38%	39%
Food safety	24%	36%	40%
Market appearance	16%	39%	45%
Lack of regulation	17%	34%	49%
Uncertain about production location	15%	37%	48%
Lacking transportation to market	15%	29%	55%
Unattractive packaging	12%	30%	58%

Note: The number of respondents is 484.

In an effort to investigate potential barriers to purchasing local products, we asked, "Which of the following possible factors limit your purchases of locally produced food?" Respondents were asked to select whether the provided factors were "very limiting," "moderately limiting," or "not limiting." Table 9.1 is ordered for visual ease. The limiting factors were randomly ordered for each individual survey respondent (and thus were not presented to respondents in the order depicted in the table).

The results from this preliminary analysis suggest that the largest factor inhibiting the purchase of local products for Indiana residents is seasonality: 41 percent said it was "very limiting" and only 14 percent said it was "not limiting." The unavailability or limited selection of local products was also selected as highly limiting, with only 22 percent of respondents claiming it was "not limiting," suggesting that a consistent selection of local products may increase consumer interest in purchasing local food. Indiana's weather doesn't exactly scream "year-round harvest," so this one isn't shocking. The state's climate puts a cap on what can be grown when—and as it turns out, people like tomatoes in January, whether or not they grow here then.

Price was selected as the most limiting factor behind seasonality. Respondents indicated it was "very limiting" about 34 percent of the time and "not limiting" only 19 percent of the time, which highlights price as a key contributor in consumers' food choices. As an attribute universally shared by all market items, regardless of type and whether we purchase them, the prominence of price in consumer decision-making is expected.

Inconvenient scheduling of farmers' markets was considered "very limiting" by 27 percent of respondents, while an additional 47 percent selected it as "moderately limiting." However, lacking transportation to markets was one of the least limiting factors: 55 percent of respondents claimed this factor as "not limiting," suggesting that physically getting to farmers' markets was not the issue for the majority of respondents.

What do all these limiting factors have in common? Inconsistency. Whether it's inconvenient scheduling, seasonal gaps, unavailable or limited variety, or fluctuation, the lack of consistency and reliability seems to be the deal-breaker for many consumers. Yet, on the other hand, the seasonality and variation in what is available may be part of the appeal for the consumers who seek to feel connected to what is growing around them. The reasons for purchasing local are varied and many, and the pandemic disruptions in supply chains have pushed even more attention onto locally grown and processed products. However, there are limitations and challenges, only some of which we've explored here in this preliminary analysis.

WORK CITED

Goldy, Ron, Joyce McGarry, and Bob Tritten. November 20, 2020. "How Food Purchasing Changed in 2020—Did We Get It Right?" Available at https://www.canr.msu.edu/news/how-might-covid-19-change-food-purchases-this -summer

Adapted from original posting as *ConsumerCorner.2021.Letter.21* (https://agribusiness.purdue.edu/consumer_corner/whats-stopping -you-from-buying-local/)

10

HOW IMPORTANT IS EACH FACTOR TO YOU WHEN PURCHASING LOCAL PRODUCTS?

BY BEN ELLMAN AND TAYLOR THOMPSON

C onsumers purchase local food products for a variety of reasons. We asked those 484 Indiana residents previously mentioned in chapter 9, "How important is each factor to you when purchasing local products?" Respondents were asked to indicate whether each of the seven provided factors were "extremely important," very important," "moderately important," "slightly important," "not at all important," or "not sure/don't know" (table 10.1).

Respondents were not forced to make tradeoffs among these factors. Each factor was ranked independently. Therefore, every factor could be rated as "extremely important" by a single respondent. As expected, since tradeoffs were not forced and respondents could place importance on a variety of factors, the most common responses were "very important" or "moderately important" for most factors studied. Two factors stand out as differing from this trend: quality and meeting or knowing the producer.

Let's start with quality. Of the provided factors, survey respondents overwhelmingly indicated that quality was the most important reason for purchasing local food products, with only 4 percent of respondents

TABLE 10.1. *Respondents' Rating of How Important Each Factor Is in Local Purchasing*

	EXTREMELY IMPORTANT	VERY IMPORTANT	MODERATELY IMPORTANT	SLIGHTLY IMPORTANT	NOT AT ALL IMPORTANT	NOT SURE
Lessen environmental impact	18%	24%	26%	19%	10%	5%
Meeting/knowing the producer	8%	11%	18%	17%	40%	5%
Quality	45%	37%	10%	4%	2%	2%
Price compared to non–locally produced items	18%	32%	30%	12%	5%	2%
Product variety	17%	33%	32%	10%	5%	3%
Supports local economy	25%	33%	24%	10%	4%	4%
Sustainability	20%	31%	27%	11%	6%	4%

indicating it was either "not important" or they were "not sure." Over 80 percent of those surveyed selected quality as "extremely important" or "very important." For comparison, the next most important factor for buying local products is supporting the local economy, with 58 percent of respondents indicating it was "extremely important" or "very important."

The data suggests that consumers differentiate based on quality; appearance, taste, smell, and other attributes likely all play a role. While quality is clearly the highest-rated factor, more research is needed on how this varies across product types. For example, a browsing consumer may value attributes of quality differently depending on the desired product, influencing how they choose between certain local and nonlocal goods. Whether consumers truly associate local products with higher quality likely depends on product type and deserves further examination.

Roughly 40 percent of respondents viewed meeting or knowing the producer as "not at all important." For some, this is just an outcome of the current market structure in which a complicated supply chain takes products from the farm gate, transforms them, and delivers them to consumers sometimes half a world away. For others, this may come as a surprise. One possible question worth exploring is the area in which respondents live. More urban regions tend to have less ease of interaction or direct access to producers. Respondents from the densest population regions more often reported lesser importance of knowing the producer. While location *may* account for some of the reason for this surprising response, further analysis is needed regarding this possibility, as well as additional demographic factors such as age, buying preferences, and household income brackets (which rated higher versus lower importance in meeting and knowing the producer).

Agriculture is more than just an industry; for many, it is a way of life. Without a doubt, it has (and rightfully so) an emotional attachment for producers. But what about in terms of the overall global market? Simply put, consumers see products before we see those who work to provide them. What's another example of this? Let's take a trip back to high school economics class. The creation of a pencil is commonly taught when describing global markets—one simple object requiring input from multiple regions and players. The same applies to various industries.

For the consumer, the desire for a quality product outweighs the need for personal connection to its origin. That's not a knock on those working hard in the industry, but merely something to acknowledge as part of our collective understanding of consumers as we shape communications and marketing efforts in our diverse and varied agricultural and food markets.

Adapted from original posting as: *ConsumerCorner.2021.Letter.23* (https://agribusiness.purdue.edu/consumer_corner/how-important-is -each-factor-to-you-when-purchasing-local-products/)

11

AN ATTEMPT AT BALANCED DISCUSSION OF TRADEOFFS SURROUNDING BUYING LOCAL

BY TAYLOR THOMPSON AND NICOLE J. OLYNK WIDMAR

---

n the not-too-distant past, buying local wasn't a trend—it was simply how we lived. The common practice for most of human existence was to grow, hunt, or gather what you could in your local geographical location and climate. However, in recent decades, we have truly been spoiled by the riches of a global supply chain.

Today, our grocery stores and restaurants are filled with options—so much so that many of us have lost the wonder of finding caught-today seafood in rural Kansas or coffee basically anywhere in the United States. Instead, we are now seeing a movement that seeks to "get back to old ways." While these nostalgic preferences are admirable, they may sometimes overlook the complexity of what these choices entail.

We aren't here to tell you what to buy, as purchasing decisions are made individually and there are many factors to consider. That being said, following are five commonly raised points in the spirit of considering the costs, benefits, and tradeoffs involved in the recent nostalgia—and market—for local.

Some of these tradeoffs associated with buying local are quite fuzzy and highly personal in terms of whether or not benefits outweigh costs, but common points of contention arise around a few questions:

1. DOES LOCAL MEAN SMALLER?

We love the idea that a small business can find its place in the market. Many people agree that it is important to support small businesses. The problem here is that the definition of small is as blurry as what constitutes local.

So, what is local? In a recent publication, we identified definitions of local for a nationally representative sample of $n = 1,200$ US residents and found that "from one's own county" was most common, followed by "home county and neighboring counties" and "within 100 miles from home" (Bir et al. 2019). In response to this inquiry, 28 percent indicated that local meant within their own county of residence, 23 percent within 100 miles or less from home, 23 percent said their own and neighboring counties, 14 percent said their home state, 3 percent defined local as anywhere in the United States, and 8 percent were unsure what local meant—even with options provided. A number of other studies have sought to understand the definition of local using miles from home, state or county lines, as well as a variety of other measures. "Closer to home" (as opposed to the further away options presented) seems to be the answer in most cases, but there's clearly no universally accepted definition of local.

Similarly, what one person considers small might not qualify as such to someone else, and this too may change depending on the specific industry or geographic location. USDA statistics show 90 percent of US farms are classified as "small" (gross cash farm income less than $350,000), accounting for 22 percent of production. In contrast, just 2.7 percent are large-scale (gross cash farm income between $1 and $4.9 million), yet they account for 43.8 percent of production (Whitt et al. 2020).

In short, a business isn't small just because it's local, and local doesn't always mean small. From a research standpoint, our interest lies in better understanding whether consumers are seeking to buy local, to support or buy from small businesses, or potentially both.

2. IS LOCAL BETTER FOR THE ENVIRONMENT?

It is very common to hear about the environmental benefits of buying local, but two points to remember and disentangle are production and transportation. These two areas are relevant to discussions about greenhouse gas (GHG) emissions in the agriculture industry. The vast majority of GHG emissions come from production, not transportation. Transportation accounts for roughly 10 percent of agricultural product emissions (Ritchie 2020).

In truth, the environmental aspects of production are broad and vary widely. For starters, what products are we talking about, and where do you live? As discussed in chapter 7, if you are buying sweet corn in Indiana, then local may indeed be better for the environment (assuming production practices are employed to take environmental impacts into account) because Indiana is well suited to produce it (we have a comparative advantage). Transportation emissions would also be limited. But it is not a given that local is always better for the environment. There are countless factors to consider, including whether the item can be produced with lesser inputs or impact elsewhere. The environmental cost of a food item is product-specific, farm-specific, supply chain–specific, and consumer-specific. As other agricultural economists have pointed out, whether local product X (or basket of goods A) is more environmentally friendly than local product Y (or basket of goods B) is an empirical question (Lusk and Norwood 2011). It isn't as simple as selecting one single production system as superior. In other words: It's complicated.

3. DOES LOCAL MEET THE STANDARDS OF A DIVERSIFIED DIET?

More simply put: Can you get everything you want produced locally?

Which diet is best—raw, vegan, keto? The number of potential diets is seemingly endless these days. No matter the diet you choose, variety is typically considered important, if not for nutritional balance then by human preference. You can get local milk in Wisconsin, but not bananas. I can get plenty of local sweet corn in Indiana at harvest time, but no local oranges. Buying local cannot match the variety, volume, and efficiency of the modern supply chain (Lusk and Norwood 2011). Now, whether your own definition of local offers enough variety to meet your preferences, taking into account seasonality, production processes, or product attributes, is up to you.

4. WHAT DO DEMOGRAPHICS HAVE TO DO WITH BUYING LOCAL?

People sure do like to talk about millennials and what they've done or not done to society. The millennial generation, in particular, has been at the forefront of the "local" movement (Rosenbloom 2018). Blend this with modern social media, and trends become widely adopted at speeds never seen before. But don't forget that millennials also happen to be 25 to 40 years old in 2021, which is prime time for rising incomes due to having progressed in their careers, having families, feeding kids, and generally having the tools and time to invest in things like cooking and eating. So, yes, millennials are at the forefront of a lot of buying decision discussions today. Are they the cause of interest in local foods rising? Maybe, but correlation isn't causation. Multiple factors are at play here. While economists are always interested in who buys what and why (because it contributes to our understanding of the market), that doesn't mean we've found *the* explanation for a growing market or societal trend.

5. WHAT HAS COVID-19 TAUGHT US (SO FAR)?

From a market standpoint, it's impossible to discuss COVID-19 without mentioning the food supply chain. You may have heard that it "broke down" or "needs a complete overhaul." Local has been suggested as a solution, especially since local meat processors were overwhelmed with demand during early pandemic surges. If we take a retrospective look at the supply chain during the pandemic era, we find a series of systems that strained and then rallied to keep quality products on shelves at reasonable prices. However, this isn't to say there weren't some painful times.

Knowing what we know now, we may suggest that agricultural and food supply chains do some introspective thought about resiliency versus redundancy. To what degree have we lost resiliency in the system by attempting to reduce redundancies and gain efficiency? Taking all of the evidence together, and with the benefit of time, the food system in the United States has proven to have more resiliency than it was given credit for in some of the earlier COVID-19 lockdown days. Granted, this does not mean there isn't room for improvement by firms involved in the food chain. There is always room for improvement, and many firms are already making investments in resiliency. This also does not mean there isn't room for the possibility of regulation or legislation to force practices and investments to improve resiliency. Indeed, there were rough days when shoppers couldn't get what they wanted, and there were times of obvious cause for concern as the system strained to keep up.

While everyone has faced pressure in the COVID-19 economy and era, the food system in the United States has provided safe and plentiful (mostly) products in the locations where it was demanded (mostly) at the time it was demanded.

Was selling local extremely valuable to many producers during COVID-19? Yes. Was buying local extremely valuable to many consumers during COVID-19? Yes. Does this mean local systems are inherently superior? No.

Local production, processing, and sales are valuable attributes of food items for many people. However, every system has tradeoffs among attributes and goods, and no system is inherently superior. This ultimately boils down to consumer preferences. There isn't a right answer, there's just your answer. And your answer likely changes depending on the day, time, price, and product.

WORKS CITED

Bir, Courtney, John Lai, Nicole J. Olynk Widmar, Nathanael Thompson, Jodee Ellett, and Caroline Crosslin. 2019. "'There's No Place Like Home': Inquiry into Preferences for Local Foods." *Journal of Food Distribution Research.*

Lusk, Jayson, and Bailey Norwood. 2011. "The Locavore's Dilemma: Why Pineapples Shouldn't Be Grown in North Dakota." econlib.org. January 3. https://www.econlib.org/library/Columns/y2011/LuskNorwoodlocavore.html.

Ritchie, Hannah. 2020. "You Want to Reduce the Carbon Footprint of Your Food? Focus on What You Eat, Not Whether Your Food Is Local." ourworldindata.org. January 24. https://ourworldindata.org/food-choice-vs-eating-local.

Rosenbloom, Cara. 2018. "9 Ways Millennials Are Changing the Way We Eat." washingtonpost.com/lifestyle. February 21. https://www.washingtonpost.com/lifestyle/wellness/9-ways-millennials-are-changing-the-way-we-eat/2018/02/20/6bb2fe60-11eb-11e8-8ea1-c1d91fcec3fe_story.html.

Whitt, Christine, Jessica E. Todd, and James M. McDonald. 2020. "America's Diverse Family Farms: 2020 Edition." ers.usda.gov. December 10. https://www.ers.usda.gov/publications/pub-details?pubid=100011.

Adapted from original posting as *ConsumerCorner.2021.Article.8* (https://www.agribusiness.purdue.edu/consumer_corner/an-attempt-at-balanced-discussion-of-tradeoffs-surrounding-buying-local/) and *Consumer Corner.2020.Letter.13.* (https://agribusiness.purdue.edu/consumer_corner/talking-about-toilet-paper-and-meat-again/)

12

LET'S TALK TURKEY

W hen it's post-Halloween—cue the Christmas music! Although, in 2021, we still didn't go into department stores anymore, so I guess I'm not sure where to cue it ... let me try again: "Alexa, cue the Christmas music!" Ah, there we go.

In any year, the moment Halloween is behind us, the winter holidays are front and center. After 2020's year of holiday adaptations from trick or treating within our own homes for Halloween, to top mentions about Thanksgiving 2020 in a national media search being "cancel," "not celebrate," "not want," "avoid," and "not eat," and capping off the year with an anxiety-laced Christmas, we were all anxious for the holidays of 2021. (Note: We did not say we were all anxious for *normal* holidays. We officially retired the word "normal.")

Next up was Thanksgiving 2021, with turkey once again as the star. And in 2021, that star came with a bigger price tag. Back in 2020, when we were experiencing the first COVID-19 holiday season, meat markets were worried about the size of the turkey. Not because people wanted bigger turkeys, but because our gatherings were so much smaller. In 2021, the story shifted. According to the October 18, 2021, *Livestock, Dairy, and Poultry Outlook* from USDA's Economic Research Service (ERS):

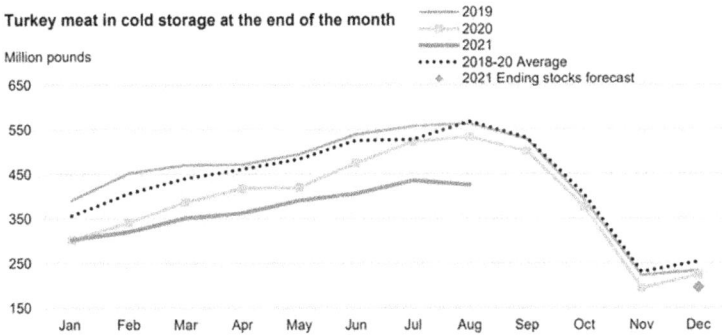

FIGURE 12.1. Turkey Meat in Cold Storage. *Source:* USDA, Economic Research Service Livestock, Dairy, and Poultry Outlook dated October 18th, 2021. Available at https://www.ers.usda.gov/publications/pub-details?pubid=102399

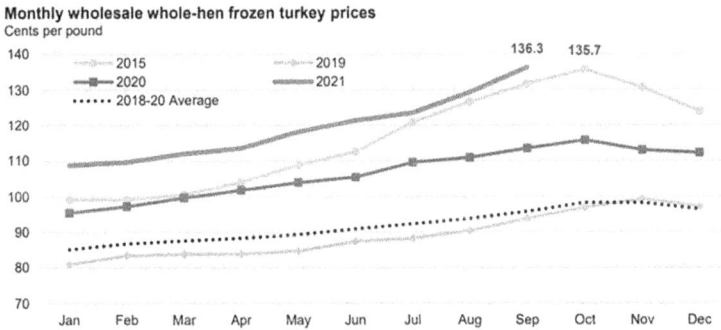

FIGURE 12.2. Monthly Wholesale Whole-Hen Frozen Turkey Prices. *Source:* USDA, Economic Research Service Livestock, Dairy, and Poultry Outlook dated October 18th, 2021. Available at https://www.ers.usda.gov/publications/pub-details?pubid=102399

Turkey production and ending stocks were adjusted down on recent data. Turkey exports were also adjusted down, while prices were adjusted up in both 2021 and 2022, reflecting lower supply expectations.

In short: Less turkey fuels higher prices. Turkey production (forecasted at the time) for 2021 was down 2 percent from 2020 according to the ERS.

Exports were also down in 2021 compared to 2020 but remained consistent as a share of total production (at approximately 10 percent).

Meanwhile, turkey in cold storage—tracked by USDA's National Agricultural Statistics Service (NASS)—follows a very predictable and obvious annual pattern in which we build up stocks of turkey all year until the fall season, then they get drawn down as retailers start to stock up for the holidays. But in 2021, storage levels were notably lower. According to ERS analysis of NASS data, turkey stocks in August were down 20 percent from August 2020. The overall pattern of 2021 is in keeping with prior years, but the total stock is lower all year, and the peak came earlier in the summer than in past years.

Of course, what people really care about is price. In September 2021, wholesale prices for frozen whole hens averaged 136.3 cents per pound—the highest monthly price since USDA began tracking the series in 2006.

If you've been following along since chapter 8 (Yes, that chapter was about chicken. Wrong bird, I know, but stay with me.), you know I'm interested in how prices vary by part of the bird—not just whole birds. So, let's look at turkey breasts. Turkey breasts are less seasonally impacted from the demand side, and while they may become more popular for various reasons, that popularity isn't as obvious and pointed as the holiday rush for whole turkeys. Turkey breasts have many more uses than being served whole, including for sandwiches, food service, and at-home dishes.

Wholesale breast prices were depressed in 2020 compared to the 2015–2019 average, likely the result of decreased demand for food away from home, subs, and sandwiches, in addition to the overall economic and market forces impacting meat markets in 2020. The 2021 wholesale breast prices started out in the 2020 range but took off in Q2 and haven't looked back. A return to food away from home, lunches out, and switching away from other relatively more expensive meats have fueled this rise alongside supply-side factors. Nonetheless, it's worth noting that while the holiday spotlight is on the whole bird in the center of the table, we cannot forget that livestock animals are not widgets and that making more of any animal product is going to have impacts on the supply of other animal products.

WORK CITED

USDA, Economic Research Service. *Livestock, Dairy, and Poultry Outlook*. October 18, 2021. Available at https://www.ers.usda.gov/publications/pub-details?pubid=102399.

Adapted from original posting as *ConsumerCorner.2021.Letter.35* (https://agribusiness.purdue.edu/consumer_corner/lets-talk-turkey/)

13

DIVERGENT MARKET MOVEMENTS ON VARYING BEEF CUTS

BY MARIO ORTEZ

U nlike some manufacturing businesses that assemble pieces into a final product, the beef manufacturing industry (like other livestock industries—see chapter 8: "Chicken Wings Come from Actual Chickens") works in reverse. It disassembles a carcass into different cuts. More specifically, beef carcasses are broken down into different primals, which are then further divided into individual cuts. The biology of cattle is such that beef cuts have very significant differences in characteristics that translate into different attributes like tenderness, juiciness, flavor, and appearance. Where specific cuts end up in the market is heavily influenced by those biological differences, along with a mix of social, cultural, and consumer preference aspects. That mix shapes where consumers want to eat them.

In the United States, the main distribution channels for fresh beef include supermarkets, restaurants, hotels, further processors, distributors, and export markets. Each of these has different preferences. Restaurants may favor certain beef cuts, and such preferences are likely different from those of supermarkets. Even more, some cuts may heavily rely on export markets for their distribution. Understanding such complex but fascinating relationships is a great first step into the world of beef economics.

Among agricultural economists, price relationships across different segments of the beef supply chain have long been of interest. For example, the price difference between wholesale beef (the price paid to the packing plants) and retail beef (the price paid to supermarkets) has allowed economists and stakeholders to understand the structure of the beef supply chain and how this structure may change over time.

In my research, I proposed a new way to study beef prices by looking at the price relationships of different beef cuts within each segment of the supply chain. The idea is that differences in cut characteristics and end uses may shed light on important economic happenings in this industry. For example, the price relationship of beef cuts within a segment of the supply chain—let's say wholesale—and its change over time may not only affect profits on the beef packer side but also influence the type of cuts a supermarket will feature at the store. This influence may ultimately influence what the final consumer chooses to put in their grocery cart.

A focus in my ongoing research (in collaboration with Drs. Nathanael Thompson and Nicole Olynk Widmar) is what happens when a disruption hits just one segment of the supply chain, such as restaurant closures. Filet mignon, made from wholesale tenderloin, is traditionally purchased at restaurants (Gibson 2020) and is the most frequently menued steak by full-service restaurants (Daley 2018) and the largest dollar generator in food service beef sales (Pawlak and Napier 2019). That means tenderloins rely heavily on restaurants for distribution to consumers, more than other beef cuts, say New York strips or chuck rolls (used for roasts), which are popular in supermarket specials. And, of course, we all remember what happened in 2020: Restaurant closures during the early stages of COVID-19 brought food-away-from-home spending to a historic low—even lower than during the 2008 financial crisis (see figure 13.1).

This disruption gave us a unique opportunity to study whether certain cuts (like tenderloins) were disproportionately affected. To study this hypothesis, we built a wholesale price ratio of tenderloins over other beef cuts to see how they have behaved over time and how they behaved during restaurant closures and COVID-19–induced disruptions overall (see figure 13.2).

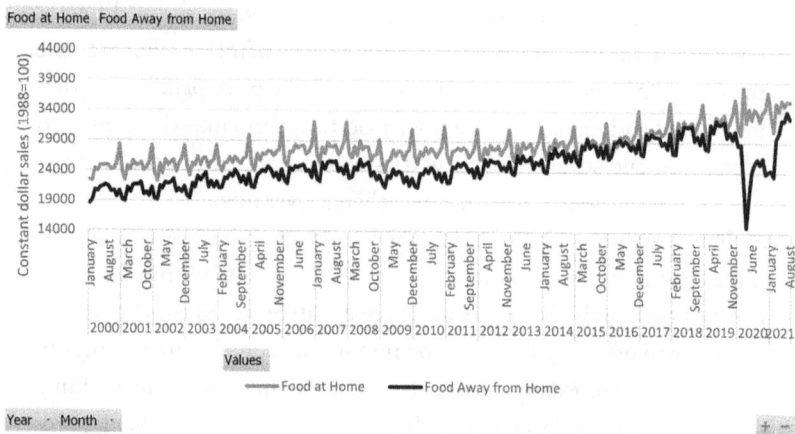

FIGURE 13.1. Food at home versus food away from home. *Source:* Zaballos and Sinclair (2023).

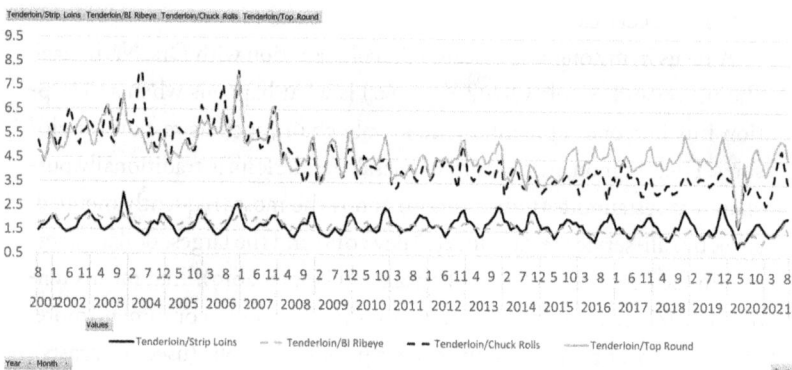

FIGURE 13.2. Choice beef price ratios: Tenderloins compared to other beef cuts. *Source:* Zaballos and Sinclair (2023).

Take the tenderloin/chuck roll price ratio (gray line) as an interpretation example. In August 2021, tenderloins traded for 3.5 times the price of chuck rolls. At the height of restaurant closures in 2020, this ratio collapsed down to almost 1.5. More generally, figure 13.2 shows that though there have been severe shocks in the beef markets over the past two decades—including BSE (bovine spongiform encephalopathy), financial crises, and widespread droughts—none of them have had such a severe effect on the price relationship between tenderloins and other beef cuts. This lends support to our hypothesis that the novelty of localized market shock of restaurant closures had a disproportional effect on some beef cuts.

The combination of factors that ultimately led to this highly unusual price relationship behavior among beef cuts is complex, but we can infer a few things from the relationship's instability during 2020. One is that retail, processors, or even export markets (which serve as alternative distribution channels for food service) were not substantially able to absorb the supply of tenderloins that usually go to food service. Another possibility is that consumers were not willing or able to purchase tenderloins in retail settings, leading supermarkets not to seek them in wholesale markets. Many other reasons could have played a role, but by 2021, tenderloins regained their proportional pricing relative to other beef cuts—which, at the time, may not have been great news for those who had taken advantage of their unusually low relative prices in 2020.

WORKS CITED

Daley, Bill. 2018. "In Praise of Filet Mignon: Maligned by Chefs Yet Still Beloved." *Chicago Tribune*, June 14, 2018. Accessed July 15, 2025. https://www.chicagotribune.com/dining/craving/in-praise-of-filet-mignon-maligned-by-chefs-yet-still-beloved/.

Gibson, Kate. 2020. "Filet Mignon Is Cheapest in Decade as Coronavirus Upends Meat Supplies." *CBS News—MoneyWatch*, April 28, 2020. Accessed July 15, 2025. https://www.cbsnews.com/news/coronavirus-supply-filet-mignon-lowest-cost-decade/.

Pawlak, Joe, and Michael Napier. 2019. "Usage and Volumetric Assessment of Beef in Foodservice." Presentation prepared by Technomic for Beef It's What's for Dinner, April 26, 2019. Accessed July 15, 2025. https://www.beefitswhatsfordinner.com/Media/BIWFD/Docs/4_26_19-2018-volumetric-summary-for-beef-research.pdf.

Zaballos, Eliana, and Wilson Sinclair. 2023. "Monthly Food Spending Remained Higher Year over Year in May 2023." usda.gov/data-products. August 8. https://

ers.usda.gov/data-products/chart-gallery/chart-detail?chartId=100407#:~:
text=Food-away-from-home%20spending%20during%20March%202021
%20through,March%202021%20through%20May%202023.

Adapted from original posting as *ConsumerCorner.2021.Letter.38*
(https://agribusiness.purdue.edu/consumer_corner/divergent-market
-movements-on-varying-beef-cuts/)

14

REVISITING FOOD AND MEDICINE TOGETHER TO IMPROVE THE HUMAN CONDITION

W ith increasing focus on human behavior in a post-pandemic era and its impact on health and well-being, concerns about food insecurity right here in the United States—especially among children who have faced precarious situations with school closures and related physical and mental health concerns—are front of mind for many of us in agriculture who seek to provide ample nutrition and food.

Thinking back a bit, we collected data in February 2016 from Midwestern households on food security status, simultaneously inquiring about chronic and acute health conditions, medical expenses, and the tradeoffs being made surrounding these two aspects of human well-being. The resulting paper, "The Intersection of Food Insecure Populations in the Midwest U.S. and Rates of Chronic Health Conditions," is freely available with Open Access in the journal *Agriculture and Food Security*.

TABLE 14.1. *The Intersection of Food Insecure Populations in the Midwest US and Rates of Chronic Health Conditions*

	HIGH FOOD SECURITY	FOOD INSECURE	LOW FOOD SECURITY	VERY LOW FOOD SECURITY
Households without children (*n* = 749)	72%	18%	8%	10%
Households with children (*n* = 360)	46%	44%	15%	28%
All adults (*n* = 1,265)	65%	25%	10%	15%

Source: Dominick et al. (2018).

Our findings mirrored previous studies in terms of overall drivers of food security status; however, we studied households of all income levels rather than focusing on those below a given threshold. By doing so, we identified a segment of households in the Midwest with seemingly ample income, but with chronic medical conditions and related expenses sometimes pushing those households into food insecurity as decisions were made to skimp on medications to allocate funds for food, or vice versa (see table 14.1) (Dominick et al. 2018). In the table, the difference in the sum of "Households with Children" and "Households without Children" and the "All Adults" categories can be accounted for by a group of respondents for whom specific household makeup could not be determined; these are known as ambiguous households (*n* = 156) (Dominick et al. 2018).

In total, being male, middle-aged, having children in the household, and/or having diabetes, an eating disorder, depression, or anxiety were significant determinants of decreased food security in our study. While the relationship between health and nutrition is known, it may not always be fully appreciated when discussing food security and nutrition alongside medical and health issues. As noted in the study: "The researchers of this study acknowledge a number of health issues can be alleviated by improved food quality and access, so addressing chronic illness as a contributor of food security can improve the metrics of food security measurement and can improve policy designed to ease food access constraints on households" (Dominick et al. 2018).

We concluded our article by saying, "Policy makers should consider how food and health overlap when measuring food security and when generating programs to alleviate it." Upon reflection and considering the situation that many US households faced (or continue to face) during COVID-19, this proved to be more timely than when it was originally written. With unemployment, cutting back hours, limited opportunity due to health considerations or chronic conditions, illnesses, and caretaking responsibilities, we need to consider the overlap between food and health policies. Given what we know about food security and children, we may wish to devote special attention to the food security and health status of children and the related situations of caretakers and household members surrounding them.

WORK CITED

Dominick, S. R., Nicole J. Olynk Widmar, Audrey Ruple, Jonathan Z. Grennell Weir, and Lalatendu Acharya. 2018. "The Intersection of Food Insecure Populations in the Midwest U.S. and Rates of Chronic Health Conditions." *Agriculture & Food Security* 7, no. 43. https://doi.org/10.1186/s40066-018-0195-z.

Adapted from original posting as *ConsumerCorner.2021.Letter.39* (https://agribusiness.purdue.edu/consumer_corner/revisiting-food-and -medicine-together-to-improve-the-human-condition/)

15

WHAT MEATS AT THE HOLIDAY MEALS?

A Look at December Holidays 2020

BY NICOLE J. OLYNK WIDMAR AND COURTNEY BIR

C onsumer meat purchasing behaviors have been a topic of significant debate in recent chapters, especially as individual products like chicken wings have dazzled the marketplace with "the best of times and the worst of times" in quick succession (see chapter 8, "Chicken Wings Come from Actual Chickens"). We've also had increasing debates around local and regional sourcing (see chapter 11, "An Attempt at Balanced Discussion of Tradeoffs Surrounding Buying Local"), alongside ongoing concerns about changing consumer behavior during the COVID-19 pandemic era (including chapter 6, "Much Ado About Dairy?").

Consumer Corner has long been studying holiday behaviors—from our interest in looking at what we serve at Thanksgiving, public sentiment surrounding various holidays, and pandemic-era adaptations surrounding holidays.

In late January 2021, we collected data about the winter holiday season spanning December 2020–January 2021. We sought to understand who gathered (or didn't), with whom, how many total people, and what they were serving or eating. We were curious whether smaller gatherings would lead to changes in what meat items were being served, especially since Thanksgiving 2020 saw challenges with too many large turkeys for too-small gatherings. In total, we collected data from a sample of 929 US households for whom sample demographics matched very closely with those of the target values from the US population as reported in the US Census (see table 15.1).

We found Christmas Eve and Christmas Day were the most commonly celebrated holiday meals, although New Year's Eve and other nonholiday family gatherings were also popular among respondents. On average, there were two to three attendees from within the household at holiday gatherings, while the number of attendees from outside the household was lower (means ranging between one and two people).

Beef was the most popular meat or protein for Christmas Eve, while ham edged out turkey on Christmas Day (although not by much), and beef again for New Year's Eve. Interestingly, chicken was served by a higher proportion of respondents than turkey for all holiday meals except Christmas Day.

Recall that in chapter 13, we were particularly interested in changes surrounding beef due to significant changes in beef cut prices in late 2020 compared to previous holiday seasons and the potential impact of smaller gatherings/scale of meals. In total, 25 percent of respondents changed their holiday protein consumption: 14 percent served more ham, 12 percent served more beef, and 6 percent served more fish or shellfish.

By following up with the 109 respondents who indicated they served more beef at holiday meals in December 2020, we learned 28 percent indicated it was because of the lower price of beef and because they were ordering from a restaurant. Only 21 percent indicated that a smaller number of attendees led them to change their entrée offering. And the largest proportion of agreement (38 percent) was a change simply due to the preference of the person doing the cooking.

Certainly, there is no denying that 2020 was "different." We have explored a variety of explanations for holiday meal differences and did find some support for the idea that relative prices or size of gatherings drove families to make changes, but the most popular reason for serving more beef was the preferences of the home chef, driving home once again that consumer (and chef!) preferences matter.

TABLE 15.1. *Demographic Information (n = 929)*

DEMOGRAPHIC VARIABLE	PERCENTAGE OF RESPONDENTS	US CENSUS
Gender		
Male	46	49
Female	54	51
Age		
18–24	8*	12
25–34	13*	18
35–44	19*	16
45–54	16	16
55–65	20*	17
65+	23	21
Income		
$0–$24,999	19	18
$25,000–$49,999	22	20
$50,000–$74,999	16	17
$75,000–$99,999	13	13
$100,000 and higher	29	31
Education		
Did not graduate from high school	2*	11
Graduated from high school, Did not attend college	27	27
Attended college, No degree earned	21	21
Attended college, Associates or bachelor's degree earned	34*	29
Attended college, Graduate or professional degree earned	15*	13
Region of residence		
Northeast	18	17
South	41	38
Midwest	22	21
West	18*	24
Household makeup	*Average number*	
Adults (over 18 years), $n = 911$†	2.04	
Children ages 0–4, $n = 751$	0.16	
Children ages 5–10, $n = 764$	0.26	
Children ages 11–15, $n = 768$	0.24	
Children ages 16–18, $n = 743$	0.13	

*Indicates the percentage of respondents is statistically different from the US Census at the 0.05 level.
† Not all respondents indicated their household makeup; n is as given.

TABLE 15.2. *Number of People Who Attended Holiday-Related Meals in December 2020 (N given in table)*

	CHRISTMAS EVE MEAL	CHRISTMAS DAY MEAL	HANUKKAH MEAL	KWANZAA MEAL	NEW YEAR'S EVE MEAL	NON-HOLIDAY ASSOCIATED FAMILY MEAL
Number of people from within household						
Number of respondents (n)	646	789	158	132	575	403
Mean	2.940	2.843	2.367	1.924	2.687	2.725
Standard Deviation	2.190	2.172	1.683	1.670	2.266	1.989
Minimum	0	0	0	0	0	0
Maximum	15	17	6	6	30	17
Number of people from outside household						
Number of respondents (n)	639	780	158	131	570	399
Mean	1.850	1.926	1.215	1.389	1.191	1.734
Standard Deviation	3.294	2.999	1.811	1.932	2.205	2.754
Minimum	0	0	0	0	0	0
Maximum	28	25	10	10	15	16

TABLE 15.3. *Meat or Protein Items Served or Consumed at Holiday Meals in 2020 (% of respondents)*

	BEEF	CHICKEN	TURKEY	HAM	LAMB	PORK	FISH	SHELLFISH	VEGETARIAN OR MEAT SUBSTITUTE	DID NOT CELEBRATE THIS HOLIDAY
Christmas Eve	27	20	14	12	1	7	6	7	4	30
Christmas Day	21	21	25	28	3	7	4	4	4	15
Kwanzaa	2	4	6	3	2	2	2	2	2	85
Hanukkah	3	5	4	5	3	2	2	2	1	82
New Year's Eve	20	19	7	9	6	11	6	7	4	37
Nonholiday Associated Special Family Meal	16	18	11	9	4	9	7	5	4	56

Note: Multiple selections allowed (*N* = 929).

TABLE 15.4. *Changes Related to Holiday Protein Consumption for 2020 Holidays*

TYPE OF CHANGE MADE	PERCENTAGE OF RESPONDENTS (%)
No, no substantial changes from previous years	75
Yes, I served more beef	12
Yes, I served more fish or shellfish	6
Yes, I served more ham	14

Note: Percentage of respondents (*n* = 929). Multiple selections allowed.

TABLE 15.5 *Reason Respondents Who Served More Beef Did So for Their Holiday Meal in 2020*

REASON FOR SERVING MORE BEEF AT 2020 WINTER HOLIDAYS	PERCENTAGE OF RESPONDENTS (%) WHO SERVED MORE BEEF
Lower price of beef	28
Higher price of usual selection	26
Smaller number of attendees led to change in preference of what to serve	21
Preference of the person doing the cooking	38
Ordering from a restaurant	28
Other	6

Note: Multiple selections allowed (*N* = 109).

Adapted from original posting as *ConsumerCorner.2022.Article.2* (https://agribusiness.purdue.edu/consumer_corner/what-meats-at-the-holiday-meals-a-look-at-december-holidays-2020/)

16

WELL, THAT'S A FASHION STATEMENT

The Pandemic Look That's Apparently Here to Stay

BY NICOLE J. OLYNK WIDMAR AND COURTNEY BIR

I n the first book of this series, we suggested redefining the standards for what looking "awful" meant in order to avoid admitting that our then Zoom-chic selves were really falling short of any pre-COVID standards.

We think the time has come to revisit our discussions from 2020 through a new lens—one colored (clouded?) by the passage of time. Can we agree that pre–COVID-19 "normal" is never coming back? It's probably time to simply live in the present, knock it off with the "return to normal," and start planning for the real-life future instead of hoping for a return to the past.

Let's take a moment to revisit 2020. All right, Zoombies—the gig is up! Welp, you look awful. And I am judging you—with cat hair on my pants and a stain of unknown origin on my shirt. My kid wiped something (food item, I'm choosing to believe) on me earlier, and it's still there. Once we worried about accessorizing an outfit, but we now have cleared the bar if we're indeed wearing pants. When is the last time you saw a zipper, let alone used one? Wow—we've come (fallen?) a long way in home-meets-work-space quarantine life working attire. There's an entire revolution coming in retail with respect to clothing, accessories, and especially formal wear. Truth be told, the massive reshaping of retail stores was underway in the United States long before COVID-19 hit, but we certainly seem to have accelerated it.

Lessened concern with appearances makes sense in light of the weight of an anxiety-inducing health pandemic and economic crisis on people's minds. How long did we go without a haircut? That look is now socially expected, maybe even positively perceived at some points in time. Will our new casual approach become the new norm? Society has gotten more casual (slowly) over time anyway, with many office settings adopting more casual attire than the once-expected suits and ties. What will come over the next few months? It's yet to be seen, but an interesting question that will impact a large variety of markets from clothing and accessories to personal grooming to basically all of retail in one way or another.

Fast forward to 2022, and let's see what the data says about casual wear and remote work. We have an update on these earlier musings: We asked US residents in the winter of 2021 to report on their personal care, clothing, travel, and food expenditures. We obtained a representative sample of 751 US residents and have summarized some key clothing spending responses in consideration of our revisiting the new work-life attire questions facing all of us in 2022. For starters, we inquired about spending on casual clothing in the fall of 2021 relative to pre-pandemic times.

The majority of respondents indicated that they were spending about the same, but for those who said they spent more, we dug into the reasons why (allowing respondents to select more than one reason). Top reasons included wanting an update (22 percent of responses), existing wardrobe being too small/tight (21 percent), and needing clothing that wasn't previously needed (15 percent). The fourth most selected reason was that their existing wardrobe no longer fit because it was too large (12 percent), and 11 percent simply reported a change in preferences/style.

Given the massive shift in working environment and progression toward casual and Zoom-on-the-top, pajamas-on-the-bottom, we also examined the responses to this question according to whether respondents' jobs could be done remotely or not. Responses included "yes," "sometimes/partly," and "no." Responses to the same question about changes in casual

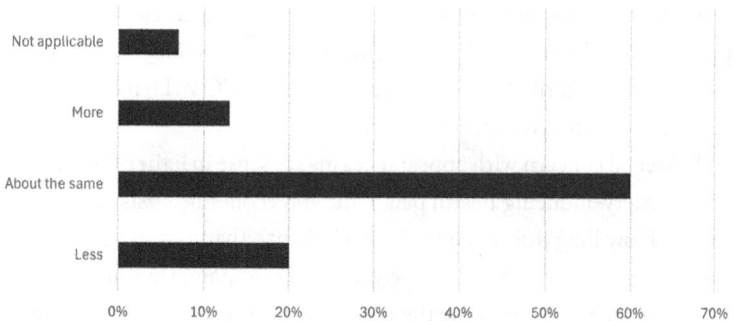

FIGURE 16.1. Spending on Casual Clothing in Fall 2021 Compared to Pre-Pandemic

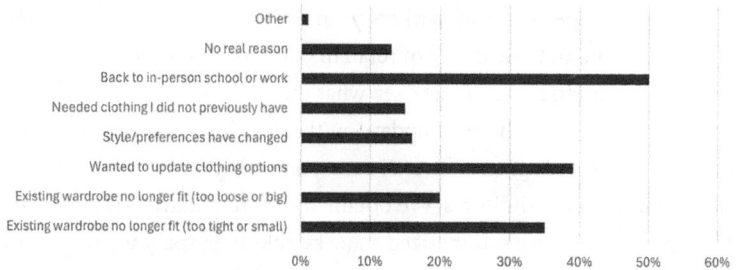

FIGURE 16.2. Reasons for Spending MORE on Casual Clothing in Fall 2021 Than Pre-Pandemic

clothing spending in the fall of 2021 compared to pre-pandemic are presented in table 16.1 according to remote working capabilities.

Interestingly, those who were able to work from home reported near-equal proportions of those spending more and less on casual clothing. Those who were not able to work remotely reported spending less on casual clothing. Of course, what constitutes casual remains in the eye of the beholder (in this case, the respondent).

We asked the same sample of respondents about spending on suits, dresses, and professional clothing in fall 2021 relative to pre-pandemic (figure 16.3).

More respondents indicated having never spent on professional clothing and about the same is still the most popular response; however, only

TABLE 16.1. *Changes in Spending on Casual Clothing in Fall 2021 According to Ability to Work Remotely (Yes, Remote Work Possible versus Sometimes/Partially versus No, Remote Work Not Possible)*

	SPENDING LESS	SPENDING ABOUT THE SAME	SPENDING MORE	NOT APPLICABLE
Working Remote	31	93	35	7
Hybrid	28	52	15	7
Working in-person	33	111	13	10

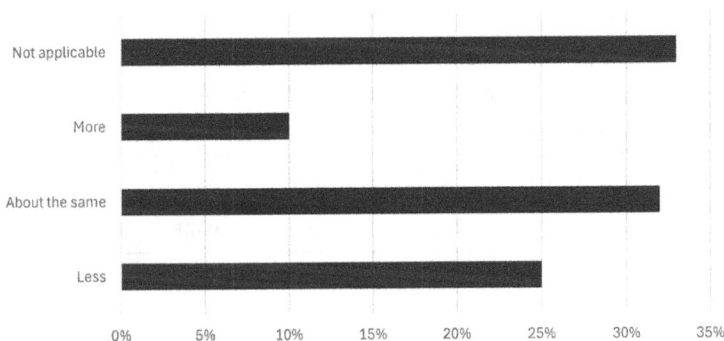

FIGURE 16.3. Spending on Suits, Dresses and Professional Clothing in Fall 2021 Compared to Pre-Pandemic

7.6 percent of respondents reported spending more for professional clothing and 24 percent reported spending less. The top reasons for those few who did spend more on professional clothing in the fall of 2021 than pre-pandemic were due to a need for clothing they didn't previously need and changes in styles and preferences.

Again, breaking out responses about spending by the ability of the respondent to work remotely, we found that a larger proportion of respondents in all categories of remote work spent less on professional clothing than the proportion who reportedly spent more.

A variety of explanations for the lack of variation in spending by remote work status exist, including overall progression toward more casual

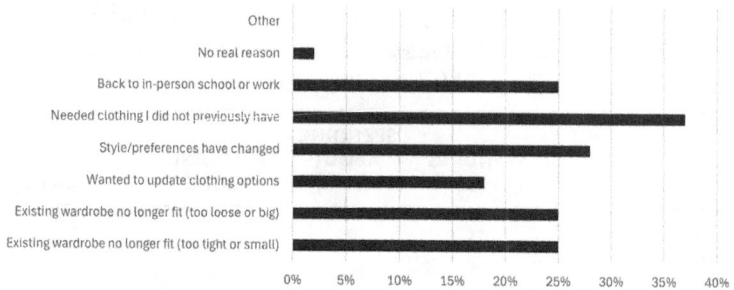

FIGURE 16.4. Reasons for Spending MORE on Professional Clothing in Fall 2021 Than Pre-Pandemic

TABLE 16.2. *Changes in Spending on Professional Clothing in Fall 2021 According to Ability to Work Remotely (Yes, Remote Work Possible versus Sometimes/Partially versus No, Remote Work Not Possible)*

	SPENDING LESS	SPENDING ABOUT THE SAME	SPENDING MORE	NOT APPLICABLE
Working Remote	45	61	27	33
Hybrid	30	44	11	17
Working in-person	37	73	8	49

wear in and out of the office environment and requirements of uniforms or specific attire for in-person work (i.e., medical professionals wearing scrubs or other professionals donning specific at-work attire potentially not captured here as professional wear of suits and dresses). Of course, just as with the definition of casual clothing, what respondents included as professional clothing remains a personal judgment call.

Spending on personal goods and clothing remains an area of interest for economists and market analysts. But household spending must also be considered in the context of supply chain challenges and inflationary pressures, especially as households weigh essentials like food, utilities, and transportation (not to mention gas prices!) against attire for changing work environments. The lasting impact of the work-from-home era is evident in our closets, our shopping habits, and even our definitions of what counts as "professional." The ripple effects? They reach well beyond wardrobes and into retail, food services, and how we define convenience and comfort in our daily lives.

———————

Adapted from original posting as *ConsumerCorner.2022.Letter.13* (https://agribusiness.purdue.edu/consumer_corner/well-thats-a-look/)

17

CONSUMERS' KNOWLEDGE AND WILLINGNESS-TO-PAY FOR WET-AGED AND DRY-AGED BEEF

BY MARIO ORTEZ

W hen you hear about aged beef, you probably think of high-end restaurants accompanied by high-end bills. You also probably think of dry-aged beef. As it turns out, the ancient practice of beef aging has two different methods: dry-aging and the less talked about wet-aging. Both aging methods have been shown to improve the beef-eating experience, and most of the beef you purchase at the store is (unintentionally) wet-aged. With the advent of online meat retailing, consumers can now purchase both dry-aged and wet-aged beef with just one click, in addition to getting this product at specialty stores or high-end steakhouses. But how much do US consumers really know about beef aging? And, aside from beef connoisseurs, are they willing to pay a premium for it?

While it is clear that consumers care most about price and palatability (tenderness, juiciness, and flavor) when purchasing beef, we don't have a strong sense of whether an average consumer cares about the method used to achieve those qualities, or at what cost. (For a study of consumer preferences for beef attributes, see our recent *Meat Science* article, "What Do U.S. Consumers Care About Regarding Beef and Its Supply Chain?" Ortez et al. [2022a]; or check out the "Monthly Meat Demand Monitor" constructed by researchers at Kansas State University [2025].)

To aid in this understanding, we recently published an article in *Q Open*, a newly launched journal of agricultural, climate, environmental, food, resource, and rural development economics, titled "Valuation of Dry and Wet Aged Beef by U.S. Consumers" (Ortez et al. 2022b). In this article I collaborated with Dr. Nicole Widmar and Dr. Nathan Thompson, both researchers within the Department of Agricultural Economics at Purdue, and Dr. Yuan Brad Kim, a premier meat aging expert with the Purdue Department of Animal Sciences. Our research investigated US consumers' knowledge and attitudes toward both beef aging methods, and, through a choice experiment, we elicited willingness-to-pay premiums for this.

Our research found US consumers are not generally familiar with either wet-aged or dry-aged beef. Over 60 percent of respondents in our study indicated they were "less than moderately familiar" with dry-aged beef and over 70 percent with wet-aged beef, making dry-aged the slightly more familiar method. Perhaps influenced by the lack of information about beef aging, US consumers generally ranked all other attributes studied as superior to wet-aged and dry-aged beef (see figure 17.1).

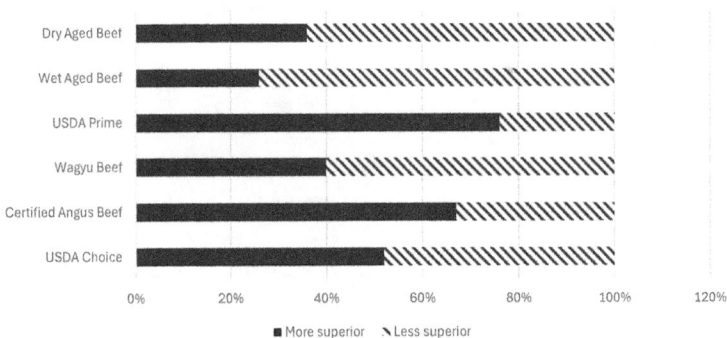

FIGURE 17.1. US Consumer Rankings of Beef Offerings

Our econometric analysis revealed that consumers' willingness to pay for aged beef is widely influenced by general beef preference (Ortez et al. 2022b). What this means is that people who already like beef generally had a higher willingness to pay for both wet-aged and dry-aged beef, which is good news given that the former is a probabilistically larger group. However, it is not entirely good news for aged beef. Although these beef-liking consumers seemed to be more receptive to beef aging, their average willingness to pay averaged $0 per pound for dry-aged beef and a modest $0.07 per pound for wet-aged beef, based on a semi-experimental setting. The fact that more familiar dry-aged beef elicited a lower premium than wet-aged beef is perhaps surprising to hear; however, we need to keep in mind that those are average premiums from all respondents.

Perhaps information campaigns aimed at educating consumers about the benefits of beef aging may help increase awareness and shift willingness to pay. Only then might the full palatability benefits of this aging practice be fully materialized for average beef consumers in this country.

WORKS CITED

Kansas State University. 2025. "Monthly Meat Demand Monitor [Survey Data]." agmanager.info/livestock-meat. Accessed 2025. https://www.agmanager.info/livestock-meat/meat-demand/monthly-meat-demand-monitor-survey-data.

Ortez, Mario, Nicole J. Olynk Widmar, Nathan Thompson, and Yuan H. Brad Kim. 2022a. "What Do U.S. Consumers Care About Regarding Beef and Its Supply Chain?" *Meat Science.*

Ortez, Mario, Nicole J. Olynk Widmar, Nathan M. Thompson, and Yuan H. Brad Kim. 2022b. "Valuation of Dry and Wet Aged Beef by US Consumers." *Q Open.*

Adapted from original posting as *ConsumerCorner.2022.Letter.15* (https://agribusiness.purdue.edu/consumer_corner/consumers -knowledge-and-willingness-to-pay-for-wet-aged-and-dry-aged-beef/)

18

CARBON MARKETS OR SOMETHING OF THE SORT

BY CARSON REELING AND NICOLE J. OLYNK WIDMAR

So, do carbon markets work, Carson?" This is the question I asked my colleague and friend, Dr. Carson Reeling, who works in environmental economics.

His reply, "I use that term 'market' very loosely, because if you are an economist who looks at these (carbon markets), they don't really look like anything that resembles a market to you."

It's a trick question, of course. Let's start by asking if they truly are markets. The answer? They're not, although there are certainly an abundance of carbon offset programs. So, let's instead call them "voluntary carbon sequestration programs." Whether a market or a program, they certainly elicited attention. With that attention comes the need for ensuring trust, transparency, and agricultural involvement.

Perhaps we should call them "nonregulatory offset programs"—distinct from regulatory markets where demand for permits and carbon sequestration would be driven by compliance rather than voluntary commitments by firms.

"This is actually a really great idea, right?" said Dr. Reeling during the *Consumer Corner Micro-Course: Consumer-Driven Changes in Ag Market*

Channels (April 6, 2022). "There's no problem with these offset markets in any real sense. From a societal perspective that's all [carbon emissions reduction] we want. We want to make sure that we reduce our greenhouse gas emissions. It doesn't matter if Walmart is doing it, or Apple is doing it, or a farmer in Indiana is doing it. As long as we get rid of those emissions, we're fine. So in principle, these offset markets should work."

Carbon trading is certainly not new. There has been talk about these markets dating back to the 1960s. We must be a little suspicious of why farmers have not been invited into carbon offsets before now.

CHALLENGES FOR AGRICULTURE IN CARBON MARKETS

There are some fundamental challenges with agriculture's role in carbon markets. Carbon markets alone have their share of challenges, too. There's a lot of demand for social action to reduce carbon emissions and for agriculture to have a role in this. There are also many challenges—technical, economic, and political—with the functionality of these nonregulatory voluntary markets. The science of all of this carbon "stuff" is not settled by any stretch of the imagination.

Our first challenge: measurement. How much carbon is actually sequestered? Measuring soil carbon is very difficult, costly, and time intensive. Current conversations often center around utilizing cover crops, which can help sequester carbon. However, the amount of carbon actually sequestered varies widely from basically zero to one metric ton per hectare per year, depending on the crop, the production practices, the cover crop, where you are, and a variety of other factors. If we are going to have any confidence regarding the amount of carbon embodied in these offsets, then we need to measure it—but that's expensive and time consuming. Due to the difficulty and cost of direct measurement, we determine carbon sequestration using models, which vary in accuracy.

Our second challenge: additionality. Or simply stated: "We don't want to pay producers for actions they would have taken anyway." If a farmer has already revealed that they will sequester carbon for free—using no-till or cover crop practices without financial incentive—then providing payment does not achieve additional carbon reductions. This undermines the credibility of the offset.

This "already doing it" acreage generates skepticism among credit buyers and society. If members of the general public are genuinely interested in carbon emissions reductions, then they are concerned that the reductions aren't "real" in the sense that no additional carbon emissions have been abated. Furthermore, the proportion of cropland in no-till or conservation tillage varies across the United States as well. We see a higher proportion of land devoted to sequestration or conservation in the Midwest. However, opportunities to expand these sites are limited.

If essentially worthless offsets are being promoted that are later discovered to have zero value, because there is a violation of additionality, and if enough people find out about these violations, then nobody will want to buy. This is a clear challenge for a nonregulatory *voluntary* market.

Our third challenge: permanence. Sequestering carbon in working agricultural lands presents the challenge that the timelines on sequestration are decades long, and a single disturbance of the soil carbon stock can release a lot of that sequestered carbon. The challenge here is that if you disturb the soil, you release the stored carbon, which is a clear problem for those who may have sold that sequestered carbon in the form of an offset.

Our fourth challenge: economics. Consumers are willing to pay for sustainability. They like labels that indicate that what they're buying is good (or at least not as bad) for the environment. But that value for sustainability by consumers is not necessarily trickling down to farmers. Surveys show most carbon programs do not provide enough compensation to justify farmer participation.

Our fifth challenge: long-term contracts and negotiations. Negotiations are taking years in many cases, and even once the contract is signed, it has an ending period that can stretch anywhere from one to twenty years. It is very unclear what happens to the carbon sequestered in the year after the contract period ends. If the practice ends, does the carbon that was sequestered get released? Who is responsible? There's a lack of clarity about what happens at the end of these contracts.

Our final challenge: liability for reversal and impermanence. Uncertainty also surrounds one-time events—like extreme weather that may release stored carbon—or permanent abandonment. Who is liable for that loss? Farmers? Credit buyers? Intermediaries? The ambiguity is problematic.

Altogether, there remains interest from all parties in carbon abatement programs (or markets, if you wish), but there also remains a number of challenges.

We have established that carbon markets are not exactly markets, the nonregulatory nature of carbon markets, and the challenges of agriculture specifically participating in carbon offset programs (or, if you still wish, markets). We've raised challenge after challenge, but given the massive public interest, many of us are left asking: If all parties seem satisfied, what's the real harm?

It seems as if everybody is winning, right? Farmers get paid. Carbon programs profit. Buyers receive offsets, and many assume those offsets represent actual carbon reductions. So why not just jump on the bandwagon and ride this out? Why are we worried about the functionality and underlying incentives beneath these carbon abatement programs? Well, because there is a lot at stake. Farmers, on the whole, have made massive strides in doing good things for the environment while growing more and more food using fewer and fewer inputs. Yet, socially we remain tense, especially surrounding environmental issues. Agriculture has very limited opportunities to participate in visible programs and get rewarded for doing the right thing. Participating in well-regulated, highly visible programs like carbon offsets can bolster the food industry's reputation, but it has to be done right.

Adapted from original postings as *ConsumerCorner.2022.Letter.30* (https://agribusiness.purdue.edu/consumer_corner/carbon-markets-or -are-they/), *ConsumerCorner.2022.Letter.31* (https://agribusiness.purdue .edu/consumer_corner/regulatory-voluntary-carbon-markets-meet

-agriculture-and-creates-questions/), *ConsumerCorner.2022.Letter.32* (https://agribusiness.purdue.edu/consumer_corner/fundamental -challenges-of-agriculture-in-carbon-markets/), *ConsumerCorner.2022 .Letter.33* (https://agribusiness.purdue.edu/consumer_corner/ag-and -carbon-markets-everybodys-winning-here-right/)

19

SEASONS CHANGE, AND SO DO OUR PREFERENCES

A t Consumer Corner, we've already taken a cue from *Who Moved My Cheese?* by Spencer Johnson (1998)—a story of how clinging too tightly to past success can leave you stuck with stale results. While the original lesson was aimed at personal growth and business leadership, its relevance to consumer behavior is just as clear. If you haven't read it in a while, you should probably do a refresher (along with your cheese).

The premise is simple: Two little people (Hem and Haw) and two mice (Sniff and Scurry) live in a maze. Everyone wants cheese, which seemingly represents success—however you define it. Sniff and Scurry don't overthink it. They just go looking. Hem and Haw, meanwhile, spend more time wondering what the cheese means, how they'll feel once they find it, and whether they deserve it.

That's lesson one: Stop complicating matters. Start looking for cheese; get going.

The second lesson, simple yet incredibly underappreciated, imparts a vital truth: Finding cheese doesn't mean you get to keep it forever. Success isn't permanent. The cheese can disappear, grow moldy, or just stop being enough. You must regularly sniff out success; it's not a one-and-done sort of thing. In the story, the mice keep their sneakers handy, so they are ready to run. Likewise, you need to keep your sneakers close. When the cheese gets old, move to find new opportunities.

And here's where we zoom out: The cheese isn't just your career or your business model. It's also the consumer. Their preferences change—sometimes slowly, sometimes all at once. While I lack a crystal ball for predicting tomorrow's demands, I'm reasonably comfortable demands will change, because they always do. Our ever-evolving tastes and preferences are not only a reflection of shifting needs and wants but also a response to options or new alternatives we didn't have before. Or, we may have fewer options and be forced to seek alternatives. We're often (almost always) unsure of what we really want. We'll know it when we see it, we say. Of course, that means that when you see something new, you may want it because it's new. However, our wants and needs are intricately tied to our stage of life or individual circumstances.

Remember the great baby formula shortage? Parents weren't demanding alternatives because they suddenly wanted a new product. They had to shift because the old cheese was gone. We also have seasonal demands that ebb and flow much like the changing seasons themselves. Think about holiday food items, for example. You only want them exactly when you want them, and you likely have very little interest in whole turkeys in June. Let's be honest: How many whole turkeys do you buy and cook outside of November? Probably not many. It's easy to respond with "that makes sense" when you're the consumer looking for holiday treats in December, back-to-school items in August and September, and turkeys at Thanksgiving. These are the proverbial low-hanging fruit, symbolizing anticipated changes in consumer demand. The first COVID-era holiday season (recall chapter 15 on holiday meals?) saw smaller gatherings, limited availability, and unpredictable behavior in the meat aisle. The cheese moved. Retailers and suppliers had to move too.

Meeting these demands is essentially forever chasing moving cheese. Sometimes, we know a change is coming, but we can't tell exactly how those changes will manifest. Sometimes, we just feel that the cheese is getting old. In both cases, staying put is the risk.

Instead of climbing to the old pile of cheese and hoping it gets better, we need to adopt the mindset of Sniff and Scurry—willing to run, willing to try. Hem and Haw, with their human hesitation, illustrate what happens when we spend too long mourning what used to work. Remember: The longer you linger by your moldy cheese of sadness, the less time you have to discover the fresher cheese ahead. At some point the fear of leaving the old cheese becomes crippling. But if you're standing in the same spot, hoping the cheese gets fresh again, you're going to miss the better cheese ahead.

Step one: Smell your cheese.

Step two: Go. Find. New. Cheese.

And preferably without too much Hemming and Hawing.

WORK CITED

Johnson, Spencer. 1998. *Who Moved My Cheese?* Putnam Adult.

———————

Adapted from original posting as *ConsumerCorner.2023.Letter.22* (https://agribusiness.purdue.edu/consumer_corner/seasons-change-and -so-do-our-preferences/?dlv-emuid=1d6c3b5c-8331-4277-9461-d2714e 9445f2&dlv-mlid=45337758)

CONCLUSION

Markets We Thought We Knew

Markets matter to everyone, because it is through markets that supply and demand determine prices for goods and services, as well as for your own time and efforts in the labor market. If nobody wants the item that you're selling, the price will go down. If many people are interested in hiring you to bring your knowledge and expertise to solve their problems, your wage is likely to increase in response to that increasing demand. Fundamentally, the market helps to allocate resources, whether they be labor or capital.

It gets said flippantly, and perhaps too often, but it would not be a conversation among economists without the phrase "Markets work" (or "the market works," if you prefer the singular). Most of the time, and to some degree, it is true. Parties come together in some format to exchange goods, services, or assets, both tangible and intangible. In doing so, they effectively arrive at a price—whether currency or otherwise. Markets drive innovation, serve as mechanisms for price discovery, and provide a way to communicate both wants and willingness to supply. Even in markets deemed inappropriate within a society, goods and services still get allocated—albeit with higher transaction costs and risks associated.

For all the efficiency created and sustained through a well-functioning system of markets, there remain challenges. There are a variety of real-world reasons why markets may struggle to function efficiently. Some of these reasons are human constructs, such as the potential for driving up transaction costs through legislating requirements or interfering in a labor market for reasons based in societal values. Other times, even extremely well-functioning markets are forced to react to external or exogenous shocks. Agriculture and food markets often face significant shocks, whether in the form of drought, disease, or shocks to demand (as when a new apple variety becomes widely popular and another is left to rot on the tree). In addition to weather or production risks, there are also transportation challenges in moving products, shortages in inputs in a given geographical region, or trade disputes limiting the ability of one country to export to another despite the presence of both willing buyers and willing sellers.

Understanding how markets react to external shocks, alongside changes to supply, demand, or policy, is incredibly important for informing policies and societal programs that help stabilize societies during impactful events. Food systems are vitally important, and everyone has a vested interest in the resiliency of food systems. A recent and extremely significant exogenous shock to food and agricultural markets was the COVID-19 pandemic. Consumer behavior changed dramatically nearly overnight. We often say that things happened overnight as an exaggeration, but in the case of the COVID-19 pandemic in March 2020, it was quite literally true. Perishable products bound for food service weren't needed, but gallons of milk for at-home consumption became scarce. Meat markets were challenged as demand shifted to retail, while supply was constrained by labor and slaughter capacity in critical areas.

There is much to learn when we look back at how markets functioned through these changes in demand, supply-side shocks, and exogenous shocks.

ABOUT THE AUTHORS

Nicole J. Olynk Widmar is an agricultural economist specializing in farm businesses and consumer decision-making under uncertainty. She serves as a professor and the head of the Department of Agricultural Economics at Purdue University.

Michael L. Smith is a research scientist specializing in the human dimensions of resource use, applying cross-disciplinary methods in agricultural economics and the social sciences. He works in Purdue University's Department of Agricultural Economics.

Erin Robinson is a communications and marketing professional with experience in agricultural business and academic research environments. As marketing manager for Purdue University's Center for Food and Agricultural Business, she develops marketing strategies, creates content and outreach initiatives, drives brand awareness, and evaluates marketing effectiveness.

ABOUT THE CONTRIBUTORS

Courtney Bir, assistant professor of Agricultural Economics at Oklahoma State University, holds a PhD from Purdue and master's and bachelor's degrees from OSU. Her research examines consumer preferences for agricultural products and production economics, aiming to align preferences with profitability. Her extension work focuses on farm finance and operational goal achievement.

Ben Ellman is a financial services professional with experience in consulting, accounting, and research on online and social media's impact across various markets. He specializes in financial modeling, managing datasets, data analysis, sports statistics, and data visualization. He currently works as a Financial Analyst in Chicago.

Lixia H. Lambert is an assistant professor in the Department of Agricultural Economics at Oklahoma State University. Her research focuses on natural resources and environmental economics, including water resource management, renewable energy systems, bioeconomy logistics, and sustainable agricultural practices.

Bailey Norwood holds the Barry Pollard, MD P&K Equipment Professorship of Agribusiness at Oklahoma State University. As a researcher, Norwood has published studies on a variety of topics, including food insecurity during COVID, the impact of wheat varieties on the taste of bread, and the philosophy of why we garden.

Mario Ortez was born into a family of coffee growers in northern Nicaragua, where he first experienced agriculture. His career spans various segments of agrifood, bridging roles in the private sector and academia. Currently, he is a faculty member at Virginia Tech, dedicated to inspiring the next generation of agribusiness leaders.

Carson Reeling is an associate professor in the Department of Agricultural Economics at Purdue University. His research is in the area of environmental economics with a focus on designing policies to manage nonpoint source pollution from agricultural lands. Reeling is interested in enhancing environmental and financial sustainability of production agriculture through an understanding of producers' participation in voluntary water quality and carbon trading programs.

Taylor Thompson is currently Commodity Marketing Specialist for the Kentucky Farm Bureau Federation. He works with farmers across Kentucky on farm policy and marketing matters for various commodities. Thompson received a BS in agricultural and resource economics from the University of Tennessee and an MS in agricultural economics from Purdue University.

Christopher A. Wolf is the E. V. Baker Professor of Agricultural Economics at Cornell University, holding appointments in the SC Johnson College of Business as well as the Dyson School of Applied Economics and Management. His research specializes in dairy sector economics.